LIVING WITH YOUR
GRANDCHILDREN

A GUIDE FOR GRANDPARENTS

Jennifer Lee
Lissa Cowan

Published by
Groundwork Press
445-5525 West Boulevard
Vancouver, BC V6M 3W6

Cover and book design by Elyssa Schmid, Radiant Design
Additional design by Lissa Cowan and Jennifer Lee

Printed in Canada by Friesens

National Library of Canada Cataloguing in Publication Data

Lee, Jennifer, 1976-
Living with your grandchildren: a guide for parents / Jennifer
Lee and Lissa Cowan.—1st ed.

Includes bibliographical references and index.
ISBN 978-0-9735444-7-3

1. Grandparenting. 2. Parenting. 3. Grandparent and child.
I. Cowan, Lissa, 1966- II. Title.

HQ759.9.L42 2007   306.874'5   C2007-900147-5

For loving grandparents everywhere

TABLE OF CONTENTS

A Journey Toward Re-parenting

Before Mary retired she had a dream of what her senior years would be like. She'd hike in parks and take brisk walks by the roadside to strengthen her aging bones. She would finally read the books her brother had given her every Christmas for the past several years. Perhaps she would sleep in, maybe even take a trip somewhere with her husband Dan during his vacation time from his job at the post office. Now just finishing up her 40th year as a nurse at the local hospital, she was looking forward to doing things according to her timetable and not working into the early hours in the palliative care ward. She would no longer be on-call, have to lift patients off their beds or spend hours at a time on her feet. So, after her retirement party, the cake and gifts, Mary went home and let out a big sigh of relief at the prospect of her new freedom.

Then a couple weeks later a call came from her youngest daughter.

"Mom, it's Anna."

"Hi dear, how are you?"

"OK, I guess. Listen, can you take Ben for a little while?"

"Why? Are you in some kind of trouble?"

"Not exactly. You see I have a chance to take a job in Winnipeg with this outfit. I know a guy there, a friend who says the pay is better than it is here. Ben's school is here and I don't want to move him again. I could stay with this friend until I find a place; I just need some money to get there."

Mary's daughter Anna was a single mom who had left an abusive relationship about two years ago. Mary and Dan had cared for their grandson Ben a few times before for short periods while Anna was battling alcohol addiction and regrouping after the relationship ended. For about a year now she'd been sober and it seemed to Mary as though her daughter was finally getting her life together.

Mary's story is very similar to those of other grandparents. The number of grandparents who parent their grandchildren has been steadily rising. According to a 2001 census, 475,000 grandparents in Canada live with grandchildren. This includes grandparents living in multi-generational households—where the grandparent, parent or parents and children reside together under one roof—and skipped generation households, where the grandparent or grandparents live with the grandchild or grandchildren and act as primary caregivers. According to the same study, there are nearly 57,000 grandparents living in these skipped generation households in Canada. This represents a 20 percent rise from 1991. Reasons for this rise are linked to poverty, teen pregnancies, parents going to prison, drug and alcohol abuse, both parents working full-time, the death of one or both parents, divorce, illness such as HIV/AIDS, child abuse and neglect. In addition, many parents simply don't have access to social supports such as daycare, legal advice or treatment for chronic illnesses, including addictions, to adequately fulfill their parenting duties.

So how did Mary respond to her daughter's situation? Well, she put her dreams of retirement on hold and did what many grandparents do when faced with a similar situation: she agreed to have her grandson Ben live with her and her husband. There are many reasons why grandparents take on the challenge of re-parenting. Some see themselves as a safety net for their families. Others fear that, if they don't take charge, the child will go into foster care and be lost forever.

Mary and Dan viewed their grandson coming to live with them as a temporary situation. They thought that once their daughter was settled in her new job and Ben was finished his year of school that he would eventually go and live with his mom. As it happened, Anna did come and take her son halfway into the summer. She started dating the friend who had encouraged her to move and accept the job in the first place and she reported to her mom that things were going really well.

Not long after Ben began living with his mom and her boyfriend, Mary went to visit them in Winnipeg. She was shocked to discover that her grandson Ben was going to school with no breakfast and wasn't properly clothed for the chilly weather. And it wasn't only that. The longer she stayed into the week, the more she suspected Anna's new boyfriend of beating both Anna and Ben. When she tried to talk to her daughter, Anna just shut her out and told her mom not to come back.

Soon after, Anna's alcohol addiction resurfaced and she once again asked her mom to care for Ben. Mary's grandson stayed with her for several months until one day when Anna's boyfriend called to say he was coming to pick up "the kid." Mary and Dan spent several hours that day on the telephone, talking to the free lawyer on the law helpline, trying to get some answers. She and her husband didn't want Ben to go back to an unstable home environment. Because Anna was drinking again, and Ben had possibly been physically abused by the boyfriend, Mary felt that she stood a good chance of securing temporary custody of her grandson. Also, Ben felt close to his grandparents and enjoyed spending time with them.

Oftentimes grandparents feel torn between trying to protect their grandchildren and helping their own children at the same time. When family relationships are strained it isn't always easy to do the right thing. But for Ben the story ends on a happy note. Eventually Anna left her boyfriend, sought counselling for her alcohol problem and became used to the idea that

Ben stayed with her mom and dad most of the time. When Mary first told her friends that she and her husband would be caring for their grandson full-time they seemed surprised. One of her friends wasn't sure she could do it given her age while another thought that Mary should let her daughter work out her problems on her own.

Although the philosophy of the nuclear family is well accepted in Canada, many families whose backgrounds are South Asian, East Asian, Aboriginal and African American view multi-generational families living in one household as the norm. In these families it isn't unusual for grandparents to assume the care of their grandchildren for extended periods of time. However, in North America, re-parenting is unexpected. People who may judge you might have had little exposure to other kinds of families, or they might doubt your ability to parent. They might think that you failed to parent your own child, so how could you be any better at parenting your grandchild?

Grandparents who find they are suddenly providing care for a grandchild or children say they often feel isolated from their peer group. While the caregiving grandparent is taking her grandchild to school or running errands for him or her, the grandparents' friends have more free time to socialize. Many of these older women and men experience financial problems and health issues as a result of their new caregiver role. Oftentimes they are filled with shame and doubt, wondering how they could have raised adult children who aren't (for whatever reason) able to parent.

A social worker came to assess whether Mary and Dan were able to adequately provide for Ben's needs. The grandparents entered into a kinship care arrangement with the British Columbia provincial government called Kith and Kin. This allowed them to apply for child benefits and have access to services that previously were unavailable to them. They were introduced to others who, like themselves, parented their children's children. This local grandparent support group even helped with childcare when the couple desperately needed respite.

As Mary's story illustrates, the road to parenting a grandchild or grandchildren is far from smooth. Whether you are a grandparent who has legal custody of your grandchildren, or whether you live in a multi-generational household with your children and your children's children, or provide occasional daycare in your own home, every situation has its own set of challenges. For those who parent their grandchildren part of the year, you must switch roles continually, becoming the parent and then falling back into the role of grandparent. You may be asked to make decisions concerning the child and then be criticized for not doing the right thing. Grandparents who re-parent face many issues in the areas of:

- Finances
- Legal
- Health
- Housing
- Education
- Childrearing
- Family.

Maybe like Mary, you also had other ideas about what getting older would be like. Maybe before picking up this book you came to parent your grandchild or grandchildren quite accidentally—just as she did—and now feel you need some guidance. If this is the case, then this book is for you.

1

Some grandparents face extreme situations. It might be a behavioural issue, financial hardship, trying to gain access to their own grandchildren, or legal issues. However, we all have one thing in common: we want the best for our grandchildren. We want to protect them and to make sure they have love and security.

—Carol, caregiver grandparent

THE CHANGING ROLE OF GRANDPARENTS

As a grandparent, you've seen sweeping and extensive changes in our society. The dawn of the Internet as well as the development of tools like cellular phones that allow us to connect to anyone, anywhere in the world with the push of a button. You've watched how families have changed, and how divorce and single parents are much more common than they were in the past. You remember how your parents raised you, and how your own grandparents played an important role in your childhood and beyond. And you watch your adult children raise their children, and you wonder what kind of memories your grandchildren will one day have of you.

A Brief History of Grandparenthood

Until recently, it wasn't uncommon for grandparents to play a much larger role in the lives of their grandchildren than we expect them to now. Grandparents were seen as leaders in the community, and as actively contributing to meeting their grandchildren's needs for roots and cultural history. In the early part of the 20th century, grandparents often lived with their adult children, helping out with childcare, household chores and other tasks. In fact, families in other countries such as India, Korea and Mexico, still live in this multi-generational family structure, which is often important to the survival of its members. The family is not just seen as a familial unit, but as an economic one where costs and duties are shared. Aboriginal families in Canada also have a strong history of shared child-rearing, and continue to practice this parenting philosophy today.

After the Second World War in Canada and the United States, cities began to grow outward, and suburbs sprang up around them to accommodate the growing numbers of nuclear families (families with two parents and two or more children). Cars and airplane travel became more affordable and accessible. Adult children moved away from the towns and cities of their youth. This created distance between grandparents and grandchildren. As well, society began to value the two-parent, two-and-a-half children household, and media from the 1950s to the 1980s reflected this in everything from advertising campaigns for cleaning products to television sitcoms, which almost always featured these kinds of families.

Developing at the same time was the idea of the free-spirited, retired grandparent. The quality of life for people in their 50s and beyond has changed dramatically. Medical advances have made many physical conditions, such as diabetes and menopause, livable and controllable. Treatments for heart disease, cancer and a host of other illnesses have extended not only the number of years older Canadians can expect to live, but also the quality of living during those years. As well, society has developed a greater awareness of health issues, and grandparents today take great care in planning their nutrition and exercise regimens. In other words, while adult children and grandchildren were developing their own, different life away from their extended family, grandparents were developing another life as well, filling their retirement years with travel, socializing and all those activities they never had time for during their working and child-rearing lives.

Grandparents Today

The result of this change in family has meant a shift in how we view grandparents. For many, the ideal grandparent is youthful, active and generous. She visits her grandchildren regularly but perhaps infrequently, and brings them candy and other gifts. She prefers to be fun and popular as opposed to the kind of grandparent who disciplines or scolds. She rarely voices her opinion on the parenting skills of her adult children, and instead offers help or advice only when asked, even if she is concerned about her grandchildren's welfare. She values the fun and responsibility-free relationship with her grandchildren and is glad to no longer be parenting in this day and age, when so many things like drugs, sexual freedom and HIV/AIDS have changed society since her children were young.

In the last 20 years, many things began to challenge the independent grandparent role. Many grandparents, who may have already felt isolated from their grandchildren because of distance and the idea that grandparents should be free and independent, began to feel intense loneliness when a number of social shifts separated them from their grandchildren, taking away the influence grandparents once had at the centre of the family where they were valued, respected and helped others. Drug addiction, particularly in young women, and the lifestyle many led to support it, left some parents unable to care for their children. Divorce rates increased and custody battles left children stuck in the middle between two parents. Formerly stay-at-home parents went back to work to make ends meet in cities that seemed to grow more and more expensive. HIV/AIDS causes the deaths of tens of thousands of people in North America every year, many of them parents.

Who steps up to the plate to care for the children left behind?

When gradually—or suddenly—your role as a grandparent changes, and you find yourself no longer acting like a free, travelling grandparent, but like a working, confused parent all over again, you may feel that there is no role model, or specific supports, appropriate for you. Because society's roles for grandparents have changed, custodial grandparents, or grandparents who take a larger role in child-rearing, are sometimes seen by others as unusual, strange and perhaps a little scary.

However, grandparents who parent their grandchildren are not at all unusual. According to the 2001 census, 475,000 grandparents live with grandchildren, either in multigenerational or skipped generation households. The same report shows that nearly 57,000 grandparents in Canada are raising grandchildren on their own. Formal and informal resources do exist, and we will be exploring them in our Resources section, as well as in other sections of *Living with Your Grandchildren.* It will take time to adjust to your new role in life, so just remember: times are always changing, but so are you. You are most certainly not alone!

THE NUMBERS

I thought I was alone with my heartache of being denied access and the challenges of raising a grandchild.
—Betty, caregiver grandparent

Between 1991 and 2001, the number of grandparents raising their grandchildren in Canada increased by 20 percent. This rise is thought to be caused by a number of factors: teen moms, parents going to prison, drug and alcohol abuse, both parents working full-time, the death of one or both parents, divorce, illness such as HIV/AIDS, child abuse and neglect.

Finances
CANGRANDS National Kinship Support, an independent, not-for-profit organization that helps grandparents who raise grandchildren, notes on its website (www.cangrands.com) that one in three skipped generation households lives on incomes of less than $15,000 per year. In a recent Canadian study by Anne Milan and Brian Hamm entitled "Across the Generations: Grandparents and Grandchildren," the authors write that in households where grandparents are the primary caregivers, 65 percent of grandparents are responsible for household finances. According to a recent report published by AARP in the United States on grandparent caregivers, 13 percent of those who are officially retired are still working either part-time or full-time. Thirty-one percent are not retired at all but are employed, full-time or part-time. Almost half have a high school education or less. Forty-five percent have some college or a college degree, and nine percent have a graduate degree.

Health
In one US study (Grinstead 2000), researchers reported chronic health problems among grandparent caregivers. Grandparents who parent their children's children have higher

levels of depression than non-caregiving peers. Some are limited in their daily activities such as climbing stairs or walking six blocks. Others feel socially isolated and experience decreased life satisfaction. More than 20 percent of grandparents who spend extended amounts of time caring for their grandchildren met the criteria for depression. This health-related topic is explored in a study called "Survey of Grandparents Reveals Stress of Caring for Grandchildren," published in 2002 in collaboration with the University of California in Berkeley, School of Public Heath and the University of Toronto.

Age
Most grandparent caregivers are in their middle 50s and over half of them have no spouse. In addition, these individuals often support aging parents along with supporting a grandchild or grandchildren. In the US, three percent of grandparent caregivers are between the ages of 45 and 49. A third of them are between 50 and 59 years of age while those from 60 to 69 are in the majority. Another 23 percent are between 70 and 79 years followed by three percent in the 80+ age group (Davies 2002).

Gender
In Canada, of the 56,700 grandparents who live with their grandchildren only, 67 percent of these were women (Milan 2003).

Special Needs
According to a study published in 2003 in the *Journal of Intergenerational Relationships* called "Grandparent-headed families in the United States" over 26 percent of children in grandparent households were seen to have emotional/behavioural issues as compared to 10 percent of children in non-grandparent households. Grandchildren in the care of their grandparents tend to be more likely to experience medical problems such as asthma, vision and dental problems along with developmental delays (Guzell-Roe 2005). Other special needs include Fetal Alcohol Spectrum Disorder (FASD), Attention Deficit Hyperactivity Disorder (ADHD), Reactive Attachment Disorder (RAD), and other conditions related to neglect and abuse.

Challenges
An AARP study published in the US, titled "The Grandparent Study 2002 Report," pinpoints the lack of adequate legal authority to make necessary medical decisions as being a top barrier for grandparents as well as a lack of medical coverage for the child. Although in Canada we have access to public healthcare and problems with making medical decisions are fewer, the challenge can be in trying to obtain things like social insurance numbers or applying for a child tax benefit on the grandchild's behalf. Other major challenges are as follows (Muldoon 2003).

COMMON CHALLENGES

Inadequate legal authority to make necessary educational and healthcare decisions, including those for Individual Educational Plans (IEPs)

Impact of costs (e.g. basic care, dental, medications, special events such as summer camps, concerts) of raising children with fixed retirement incomes

Securing child care for working grandparents with pre-school grandchildren

Legal costs associated with custody reviews

Aging and physical fatigue

Reactions from friends and society at large

Frustration dealing with the court system (e.g. lack of lawyers, affordable legal advice)

Lack of government recognition and minimal public awareness of issues

Inadequate program knowledge and training among teachers and counsellors on the specific needs of grandparent caregivers

Inadequate knowledge of available educational assistance and support programs

SOCIAL ISSUES

My challenge is dealing with the anger I feel towards people who have children and then abuse them, or decide that, for now, they don't want the responsibility of raising that child.
—Karen, caregiver grandparent

Perhaps your adult child is unable to adequately care for your grandchild or perhaps one or both of your grandchild's parents have died. Or, your son or daughter may be going through a messy divorce and custody battle, and you've stepped in to provide some consistency and stability for your grandchild. You are one of many Canadian grandparents who have come forward to take care of their grandchildren. Of course, this begs the question: why are so many parents unable to care for their children?

Poverty

This is the number one reason today why children go into foster and kinship care. Adequately attending to a child's needs includes providing him with food, shelter and clothing, and many Canadian parents struggle to make ends meet. Programs to assist parents with daycare and other expenses often do not address the needs of many families, leaving parents to face the possibility that their children will be taken into government care, or that the care of their children needs to be managed by someone else, often a grandparent.

Drugs and Other Addictions

Illicit drugs (cocaine, heroin, methamphetamine) are not new. The founder of psychoanalysis Sigmund Freud used cocaine. Opium use was at its peak in the first few years of the 20th century. However, since the crack cocaine epidemic of the 1980s, when the media was drawing attention to children of addicts (called "crack babies" by many reporters), child welfare agencies across North America have been paying closer attention to the parenting skills of drug-addicted women. Some drugs, such as methamphetamine or "crystal meth" are readily available and relatively inexpensive to buy, and are therefore more attractive to young people who are looking to experiment.

Once addicted, many women, and men, find themselves involved in high risk activities like prostitution, drug dealing and stealing in order to pay for their addictions. Children of addicts are often neglected while the parents are experiencing the effects of their drug of choice, or are searching for a way to buy another hit. Sometimes, these children are also abused, taking the brunt of their parents' frustrations with addiction and poverty. Because of the increased media attention and general awareness of the effects of illicit drug use, social workers across North America have been apprehending more children because of parental drug use and taking them into foster or kinship care.

If you are caring for a grandchild whose parents were involved with drugs, it's important to examine how you feel about drug use. While you may be angry at your adult child for endangering your grandchild and passing on the responsibility of parenting on to you, it's vital to not blame him or her, particularly when discussing his or her drug use with your grandchild. Your adult child is a very real part of your grandchild's history and identity and by blaming the parent you are also in part blaming the child.

Parental Death by HIV/AIDS and Other Causes

In 2003, approximately 1.3 out of every 100,000 Canadians died of AIDS-related illnesses ("Age-standardized mortality rates by selected causes" 2004). These deaths have left many children, some HIV-positive themselves, parent-less. Some children lose their parents to accidents, to other illnesses like cancer, or, if their parents were living high-risk lives, by violent means. This is a particularly difficult situation for grandparents; they are grieving the loss of their child while at the same time providing comfort and daily necessities to their grandchildren (please see section on grief and loss in Your Grandchild's Emotions, page 25).

Child Welfare Policy

Child welfare agencies are apprehending children much more now than before. Yet rather than placing children in foster care as soon as a parenting issue such as poverty or abuse becomes apparent, social workers are now searching for alternatives such as kinship care which entails placing the child in the home of a relative or family friend. There are two reasons for this. First, research has shown that children do much better when living in the home of someone they know and trust, and who represents stability. Attachment problems are less prevalent, and the children have fewer social and academic issues.

Second, placing a child with a grandparent or aunt or cousin represents a significant cost saving to the government. Some Canadian provinces like British Columbia and Ontario offer some financial assistance to grandparents caring for a grandchild, but these payments are usually significantly less than the payments foster parents would receive. And often, grandparents do not wish to draw attention to themselves when parenting their grandchildren for fear that they will lose custody; consequently many grandparents receive no financial help at all.

Divorce

In the event of divorce between parents, a grandparent may care for a grandchild part-time, an arrangement that can sometimes lead to full-time. However, when sole custody (in the absence of child protection concerns) is awarded to one parent instead of joint custody to both parents, the grandparents' access to grandchildren is often not even considered. When one parent is cut out of the parenting duties, the grandparents on that side are often also cut out. If you care for your grandchild during a divorce and suspect that sole custody, not joint custody, might limit access to your grandchild in the future, it is important to voice your views to your son or daughter, if possible, as well as with a legal advisor.

OTHER CAUSES OF KINSHIP CARE

Teen pregnancy   Poverty   Mental illness   Incarceration

THE STAGES
OF GRANDPARENT CARE

Watch and Worry

You begin to notice that the parents of your grandchildren are in crisis. Perhaps a daughter is having a hard time providing for her child due to unstable work. Perhaps a son is using drugs and not coming home most nights. Your grandchildren do not look happy or well-cared for and their teachers and neighbours are beginning to express concern. You worry.

Taking Part

A child protection worker conducts a home visit and your adult child calls you in a panic. You start to provide emotional, financial and practical support, hoping that, with your help, he or she will turn the family's life around. You may call more often and ask how the children are keeping up at school. Questions like this lead you to ask more as you try to find out exactly how your adult child is doing. Perhaps you pay for your grandchild's schoolbooks or agree to help out with groceries each month. You may decide to bring over a cooked dinner every week to help out.

Part-time Childcare

You offer to take your grandchildren for short visits, and sometimes keep them overnight. This gives the parents a short reprieve, but you notice that the children are anxious when the time comes to return home. Also, when you pick them up for their next visit, they are often acting out, or behaving strangely. You begin to take the grandchildren for extended periods, such as spring break or summer vacation. During these times, you hope that the parents will find a job, mend their relationship, or wean themselves from an addiction. You work to bring up the confidence level of your grandchildren, or you implement a routine that helps them with behavioural problems. However, once they have been back home with their parents for a while, their problems resurface.

The Breaking Point

The parents ask you to care for your grandchildren full-time, or you decide that the children will be better off with you, so you offer to live with your grandchildren as their primary caregiver. Or, a social worker asks you to temporarily take over the care of the children while the child protection authority investigates the family. Once you've had the children for a while, you start to feel worried, anxious and afraid. You wonder what the future holds for you and your family.

Support and Self-care

Your savings have been depleted buying necessities for the family. Your apartment is too small to fit you, your spouse and the children. You jump every time someone knocks on the door, afraid that child welfare authorities have come to take your grandchildren away to a strange foster home. With all the stress and physically demanding tasks you need to perform, your health begins to worsen. You need support and resources that will help you parent your grandchildren and deal with your swirling emotions.

You find a support group of grandparents in similar situations and you begin to feel as if someone understands you again. You have made steps to secure custody of your grandchildren and are now planning for the future, which includes taking good care of yourself to ensure that you will be ready and able to see your grandchildren into adulthood. You have found some extra cash, either through government payments or applying for a reverse mortgage. On good days, your grandchildren are the joy in your life and you feel like you have a purpose.

2

We suddenly had two children in diapers, one on formula, and very little time to prepare. The energy drain was enormous; the children would go to bed at 8:00pm, we'd go in at 8:02!
—Ralph and Barbara, caregiver grandparents

HOW DO YOU FEEL?

We had to come to terms with a feeling of mourning when we realized that the child we loved and raised, the mother of our grandchildren, is a virtual stranger to us, a stranger whose thinking and behaviours are foreign to us.

—Val, caregiver grandparent

At times, parenting grandchildren can be an emotional rollercoaster. There's the stress of watching your adult child struggle with his or her challenges, whether it be alcohol addiction or another issue that makes her or him unable to adequately parent. These past and present hurts often take a long time to overcome. The period of adjusting to your grandchildren is often weighed down by unanswered questions, such as how you'll pay for basic daily expenses like food and clothing. You may be having trouble disciplining your grandchildren. You may feel frustrated because they don't listen when you ask them to do things. This might make you feel incompetent as a caregiver, which can be quite overwhelming. You might feel ill-equipped to deal with the many issues that parents need to know today about sexually transmitted diseases (STDs), drug use, and bullying. Many grandparents worry that their teen grandkids will be negatively influenced by their peers and become drug users or partake in criminal behaviour.

Another worry that grandparents often have is that the parents may come back to demand custody or that childcare services might decide to place the children with another family. And, what if the grandparents become sick or don't live long enough to care for their grandchildren? Changing situations can greatly disrupt your emotional, physical and psychological well-being.

Feelings of Guilt

The collapse of one's family can create doubt about one's own ability to care for children. Feelings of shame, guilt and anxiety surface as you wonder whether it was your parenting that resulted in your adult child's inability to parent. Because grandchildren often come into care due to divorce, prison, child abuse, or drug addiction, grandparents often feel shame. Many questions arise. What did I do wrong? Will I get it right this time? There's also the grief you may feel for the experiences you should be having at this age such as travelling, socializing and reaching retirement.

STRATEGIES

Remember that **what happened in the past can't be changed.** The best you can do is provide your adult child the level of support you're comfortable with, and allow him or her to sort out his or her own life.

Keeping a healthy distance is perhaps the greatest difficulty for parents. But if you're the parent of a son or daughter with a drug or alcohol addiction, he or she will only accept help when he or she decides to do so.

Take time for yourself each day to just sit quietly. Maybe you'd like to make yourself a cup of tea and read a book or favourite magazine. Even if it's only 15 minutes to start with, it's important to give yourself time to recharge and connect to how you are feeling on any given day. It's also important not to sweep any emotions of guilt or shame under the rug, but to see them for what they are and accept them. Doing this may help you to lessen pressure on yourself.

Talk to someone you trust such as a good friend, family doctor or clergyperson about feelings of guilt, frustration, and worry. Communicating to someone you depend on can ease your stress and anger and alleviate the need to lecture your adult child. Be aware of negative words and expressions that place blame on you or others. Ask for help from a professional counsellor. Family based support services, community centres or public libraries sometimes offer these services on a sliding scale fee based on family income.

Social Isolation

Grandparents who parent their grandchildren often feel isolated from their peer group and from society in general. Friends might not understand why you took on the difficult task of raising your grandchild. Some might doubt your ability to parent. You might feel anger over your loss of freedom. Many grandparents express that they feel different from other families. You might see this play out when you attend a school meeting with parents and someone assumes you to be the child's mother. Explaining the situation to a stranger is complicated and so you might choose to say nothing. To the other person you could come across as being unfriendly or distant.

Perhaps your grandchild had been diagnosed with HIV as a result of his mother's drug use. Or, perhaps your adult child has an alcohol addiction. It's not easy to talk about issues like these as there's still a stigma attached to them in our society. For this reason you might choose to isolate yourself socially from friends and from pursuing other social engagements. When friends ask you to come out for coffee you might find excuses so you don't have to answer any questions about your situation.

STRATEGIES

When going through stressful times all humans need someone who understands and empathizes with them. Although being on your own might cause you to feel better at first, the truth is that **isolating yourself from others will only make you feel more alone** and misunderstood in the long run. In addition, isolating yourself socially can signal a rise in stress that could negatively influence physical and mental health. That's why it's important to meet other grandparents in similar situations.

Many cities have a grandparent support group of some kind whether it be five or six grand-mothers who get together once a month in someone's kitchen, a more formal group led by a professional counsellor or social worker, or an Aboriginal talking circle.

Rural communities often have these groups as well, though at first glance it may be more difficult to locate them. These groups, which may cover a large geographical area, may be **online on a discussion forum on a website**, or their meetings may even be conducted by telephone.

If you find that there isn't one in your area you can access you might wish to inquire at the **local community centre, Aboriginal friendship centre or senior's day centre** after other grandparents you can share with. Maybe you can even enlist them to help start up a support group!

Mental and Physical Health

It's a fact that parenting a second time brings with it a host of stresses that, when not acknowledged and resolved, can lead to ill health. Grandparents say that re-parenting brings with it a deep feeling of pride and satisfaction. All humans regardless of age need someone to love, something meaningful to do and something to hope for. Many grandparents say they've found these things through spending more time with their grandchildren. They also talk about feeling useful, which gives them better health and a desire to wake up each morning and greet the new day. Yet, the other part of this story is that these grandparents also report greater fatigue followed by a decrease in mobility such as climbing stairs, walking six blocks or working for pay. Some may experience increased anxiety with a desire to *take the edge off* through smoking and drinking more alcohol than usual. Others may experience headaches, fatigue, and increased blood pressure. As we age, health problems such as diabetes, high blood pressure and high cholesterol become more common. Many grandparents who parent their grandchildren suffer from one or more of these health problems. This not only impedes one's ability to enjoy oneself, but also causes our emotions to get the better of us. We react to this lack of wellness through our emotions by experiencing feelings of sadness, anger or frustration. Our physical and emotional states are linked in a very real and complex way.

STRATEGIES

When we're overwrought, eating and exercise play a significant role in making us feel less so.

Cut down on processed foods such as potato chips and Kraft dinner, and opt instead for chicken with salad or rice and vegetables.

Drink plenty of water and add more fruit and vegetables to your diet. Foods that are high in fat can increase your chances of developing diabetes, cancer, and heart disease. Eating more natural foods will boost your energy and contribute to a sense of well-being.

It's important to try and **stay active** while also taking time out to relax each day. Take a brisk walk to start. Walk to the corner store and climb the stairs to your apartment instead of taking the elevator.

Go for regular check-ups to the doctor and don't be afraid to see a counsellor if you feel yourself becoming depressed.

Set limits on what you can and can't do and learn to say no to yourself and others if there are already too many things on your plate. If you want to clean the house from top to bottom and care for the grandchildren, maybe you should settle on one housework activity instead. That way you'll decrease your stress level and not be so frustrated or angry with yourself that you didn't do what you set out to do. Ask yourself: What's the worst thing that could happen if I don't do this? Mostly, the answer isn't as catastrophic as you might think!

Don't be afraid to ask for help from a friend or daycare provider when things get rough.

For more details on health and stress, please see Chapter 7 in Part 2: Care for the Caregiver.

Finances

As you grow older and reach retirement age you're supposed to have fewer and fewer expenses. Your children have grown; you don't need any more furniture, and your pension just covers your day-to-day living costs. At these times in our lives people are usually slowing down, not looking for more work to pay the bills. But instead, you find that you have bills from your grandchild's medical condition, or you've been asked to pay for his softball equipment and his new pants for school just got a hole in them. A significant increase in expenses can take its toll on your emotional well-being and cause you to feel overwhelmed.

STRATEGIES

If you're a younger grandparent you might want to explore ways that you can secure more income through **working a different job**.

Try making lists of what you need to buy and how much money you have, just so you don't feel as if your finances are getting away from you. Budgeting can be scary, but it helps with the uncertainty of not knowing where your money is going.

Look for charitable organizations that sell used but like-new children's clothes, furniture, toys, and sports equipment.

Contact the government office that deals with child and family issues to see if you're eligible for a monthly child's allowance through a kinship program. And don't be afraid to use food banks.

For more information on finances, please see Chapter 5 in Part 2: Systems.

Relationships

Taking on parenting in your senior years can put tremendous strain on a marriage. It could be that your spouse doesn't agree with the child-care arrangement you've made with your son or daughter. He or she may feel resentment toward you, or you both may feel anger toward your adult child for robbing you of your former, quieter lives together. It could be that you grieve the loss of your former grandparent-grandchild relationship as well.

Sometimes parents make promises to children that they can't keep. Seeing the constant disappointment of the children you live with can be very frustrating and cause you to become angry with your adult child for being so irresponsible. A parent may take the child for a weekend and expose the child to things such as drug use or physical and verbal abuse. When the child is dropped off you may sense what has happened and feel a strong mix of sadness and anger.

STRATEGIES

When feeling frustrated with your spouse **it's important to talk** about it to him or her. Children sense when there's a problem and often they'll blame themselves for your disagreement.

Create a special time for the two of you without the grandchildren. Setting guidelines with them and being clear about why you both need time alone will enable you to diffuse your anger toward them. In turn they will come to understand that they're not to blame.

As a parent it's hard not to feel responsible for your adult child's troubles. The good news is that your grandchild or grandchildren are with you now. This means you have a chance to make a positive contribution to their upbringing, be a role model in some way. It could be that, because you haven't parented in a long time, you forget some things about being a parent. If you're feeling a need to **brush up on your parenting skills** check out what's available at your local community centre. You'll be surprised to discover that many parenting classes are subsidized. This means that either they're free or that the cost is on the low end of the scale (i.e. $15 or less). Parenting classes go from infancy to teenage years and explore various kinds of parent stress such as behaviour issues or communicating with teens. Some classes discuss topics such as how to build healthy relationships with your grandchildren or tips to help stay connected and enhance the child's self-esteem.

Be clear in your communication to your grandchildren.

Look at the role emotions play to determine how or when to use a particular form of communication. As a caregiver and role model you have a great influence on how children learn to cope emotionally. That means that learning to have a positive emotional impact on them goes a long way in helping your children's communication and emotional skills develop in a healthy way.

YOUR GRANDCHILD'S EMOTIONS

It takes a lot of patience, more patience and unconditional love to help the child to feel good about her or himself. The child needs to know, and this needs to be continuously reinforced, that it is not his or her fault that Mommy and Daddy are unable to raise them.
—Karen, caregiver grandparent

When children have experienced rapid and unpredictable change and have pasts that may include abuse, neglect or drug and alcohol addictions, it's no wonder that their emotional lives are turned upside down. Unlike adults, however, children have a much more difficult time expressing how they feel and how those feelings are affecting their everyday activities and thoughts. Young children may act out by clinging to their grandparents and having violent tantrums when separated from them. Older children may simply refuse to accept direction from you and may be uncontrollable in the classroom. Teenagers sometimes act out by having many sexual partners, or through smoking marijuana to dull the internal pain they might be feeling. Learning how to interpret these signs isn't easy, and neither is dealing with the root emotions. However, it is always worth it to try and get to the bottom of your grandchild's feelings, which are most likely complex and frustrating. After all, the last thing you want is for your grandchild to grow into adulthood with painful memories and emotions that are unresolved.

Grief and Loss[1]
The ramifications of loss on children who have lost the daily presence of their parents

---

[1] Much of this section is taken from *Adoption Piece by Piece: Lifelong Issues* (2003) published by Groundwork Press and available at www.groundworkpress.com.

(even if they were abusive or neglectful) can be devastating. If not resolved at an early age this emotional distress can lead to depression, attachment issues, substance abuse, and suicidal tendencies.

When children are moved from one home and caregiver to another, they feel a heightened sense of vulnerability. They often experience feelings of futility, and a loss of self-esteem. Questions like "Who will keep me safe?" often run through the child's mind. In John Bowlby's three-volume work called *Attachment and Loss* (1971) he writes that children grieve as deeply as their elders. Understanding and acknowledging this reality is a vital step toward giving grandchildren the understanding, support and attention they need to work through the grieving process.

When an adult experiences a loss, either through death, distance or divorce, his or her world is reduced. As a child or adolescent, this experience is compounded because there is often a greater sense of being disoriented, helpless and alone in the world. The child may harbour fantasies that her parents will come back to live with her. Though, no matter how intense, the child has difficulty talking about these feelings.

COMMON FEARS

The following is a list of fears resulting from loss during childhood.

Fear of losing the other parent
If death has removed a parent from a child's life, the child may see the remaining grandparent as a candidate for a similar fate.

Fear of going to sleep
A child may be afraid of going to sleep because she equates sleep with loss or death. Also, sleep can separate the people in the home from the child who is sent to bed while the activity in other rooms continues. The awake, mobile family can be perceived, by the child, to be deserting the sleeping child who is in the dark in an isolated environment.

Fear of being separated from the grandparent or sibling
The child may fear being left with a babysitter or being required to go some place unaccompanied by a grandparent, older brother or sister. The fear of separation can be drastic and long-lasting for the child who has experienced a loss.

Fear of being unprotected
Because the child feels that she has been deserted there is a feeling of being no longer protected. For a young child this can be quite terrifying.

COMMON FEARS

Fear of sharing his or her feelings with others

The fear of sharing one's feeling is often stronger in the adolescent. If the adolescent shares her feelings the status quo may be upset. A family member may not understand and may have an opposite reaction to the child wishing to share feelings. Often children keep their feelings to themselves for fear of hurting a family member (Staudacher 1987).

Supporting Your Grandchild's Feelings of Loss

The way caregiver grandparents respond to a child's feelings of loss is a critical factor for how well the loss is eventually resolved. It is important that grandparents accept and listen to the child's feelings, even though they may not necessarily correspond to their own feelings at the time. Saying things like "You shouldn't feel that way" or "That's not the way it is at all" undervalues the child's emotional state and sets back her process of healing.

Sometimes, your grandchild may express a desire to go back to her parents to live. While you know this is an unrealistic request (your grandchild may know this as well, deep down), try to ask your grandchild why she feels this way. You may find that she feels that she has betrayed her parents, or that she worries about their whereabouts and well-being. Give her all the facts that she can handle, tell her where her parents are and how they're doing in a way that's appropriate to her age and developmental level. Assure her that by living with you, she is no way betraying her parents, but in fact helping them by giving them the space to deal with their problems. Explain, in a way she can understand, the very practical and concrete reasons why living with her parents isn't possible. Steer clear of saying things like, "You can't live your mother because she messed up her life." Instead, use reasons that are tangible like, "I know you love your mother, but you can't live with her because she has a mental illness and needs time alone to get better." Or, "It's been hard for your father to find a job and he can't afford an apartment big enough for the two of you right now."

It is important to allow the child the freedom to grieve, otherwise her feelings won't have anywhere to go and will remain bottled up. If grandparents urge the child not to dwell in the past, this may cut off an opportunity for the child to share her feelings. These emotions will then remain tied to the past and the child's energies will in turn stay tied to her parents or previous caregivers, meaning that other areas of living, such as forming other, loving relationships with new caregivers, friends or relatives, will be impeded.

Often, grandchildren living with their grandparents may feel conflicting loyalties. They may think that they are expected to give up the memory of the birthparents or of a previous caretaker. Or they may even blame their grandparents for taking them away from their parents, regardless of how poor their parenting skills were. In Helping Children Cope with Separation and Loss *(1982), Claudia Jarratt writes that it is important to let the child know that quite the opposite is true. She writes, "The more distinct the two relationships are kept, the more the new one is likely to prosper."*

Perhaps you can **help your grandchild create a memory book**, one in which she can glue in old photos and other mementoes she may have kept from her previous home.

You can encourage her to **write down her favourite memories**. You, as the grandparent, could also contribute, adding your own photos and memories of your adult child.

Even if the current relationship between you and your grandchild and her parent is strained, it's important for you to **acknowledge that the relationship was and will continue to be an important one for your grandchild**.

Abuse and Neglect[2]

Because your adult child may be dealing with addictions or a mental illness, your grandchild may have experienced abuse and neglect, either from his parents, or from other adults in his previous home. In this situation, your grandchild may have difficulty dealing with his emotions in a way that most people would consider acceptable. He may act out by physically hurting another child or you; he may be a bully on the playground. Although these behaviours are harmful and alarming, they are your grandchild's way of expressing his pain. With his parent, he may have learned that hurting others is the only way of communicating emotion.

It's important for you to make your home feel safe for your grandchild. This way, he will be better able to express his feelings to you in a less hurtful way. Here are some tips to help communicate with a vulnerable grandchild, although keep in mind that children who have experienced abuse or neglect can always benefit from counselling and it's important for you to talk to a professional. Start with your family doctor, family centre or social worker.

---

[2] Part of this section is taken from *Adoption Piece by Piece: Special Needs* (2003), published by Groundwork Press and available at www.groundworkpress.com.

Talking About Abuse and Neglect

Accept what your grandchild tells you. You may not agree with your grandchild's opinions or version of events, but it's more important for your grandchild to feel safe in telling you anything, even if it's exaggerated or difficult to listen to.

Put aside your feelings and remain calm. You may be embarrassed, shocked, disgusted, angry, or scared by the things your grandchild is telling you. Your emotions are important too, but in the moment that your grandchild is communicating his thoughts or experiences or feelings to you, it's vital for you to delay your emotional reaction until you can deal with them on your own or with another adult. If your grandchild is afraid of how you might react, he may never tell you anything.

Emphasize that all feelings are okay, even the scary ones. However, make sure that your grandchild knows that there are appropriate and inappropriate ways to express them. The best way to teach this is by modelling healthy verbal and nonverbal ways to express feelings, while explaining to your grandchild what these expressions are and how they work. A healthy way to express feelings verbally would be something like "I'm feeling frustrated about the day I had at work." Non-verbal expressions could be if you put your hand on the child's shoulder or pat her back to show affection. If your grandchild exhibits unacceptable behaviour, make sure there is an immediate and appropriate consequence (please see Chapter 2 in Part 2: on Parenting Skills for more on this).

Self-esteem and Feeling Safe

Set your grandchild up for success by allowing him to make decisions about his own life. This helps with self-esteem and gives the child an opportunity to see that he can control positive outcomes. Allow your grandchild to set limits on safe kinds of touching. You can even write out a list with your grandchild of good touching (i.e. hugging, holding hands, kissing on the cheek and forehead, etc.). This is most effective when you provide an example and show your grandchild that you can touch your friends and other relatives in a loving and safe way, perhaps through hugging or stroking an arm.

It always helps if **your grandchild knows he is not alone.** There are play and support groups for children who have been abused and this kind of social interaction, where he feels like just one of the crowd, can help with his feelings of isolation.

Praise your grandchild for initiating safe and appropriate touching and behaviour. You can say things like, "That was a nice hug you gave me. It makes me feel loved. Thank you." Or, "I'm glad that you kept your temper when Noah took the stuffed bear away from you. You did a good job telling him you weren't happy instead of hitting him. I'm proud of you." Praising your grandchild makes him feel good so try to praise him whenever you can, if it's appropriate to do so.

If your grandchild is afraid that his abusive parent may come back for him or that the parent can still somehow, control his life, **reassure him that he is safe with you in your home** and now that you are taking care of him, you will not allow him to be abused.

Sorting Out Feelings

Children who have been abused by caregivers often have conflicting feelings. They both fear and love their abuser. If they've been sexually abused, it may be that the abuse felt both painful and pleasant. **Listen to every feeling your grandchild talks to you about**, never judging or showing surprise. Explain to him that this confusion is typical of children who have been abused, and that abusers often use these seemingly opposite feelings to control the children they hurt. Loving an abusive parent is not wrong or shameful.

Talk to your grandchild about how the human body is made for touching and feeling, just not for the kind of painful touching he experienced when living with his parents.

Define acceptable behaviour for your family and home. You can start a discussion by saying, "In our house, grown-ups don't hit kids or touch their private parts. And kids aren't allowed to do these things either."

Attachment[3]

When children have experienced major upheaval in their lives and have lived through abuse and/or neglect, they often have difficulty attaching to new caregivers (please see Chapter 4 in Part 2: Special Needs for a definition of attachment and bonding) because they have learned that trusting the primary adult in their lives only leads to unpredictable and hurtful consequences. In this situation, your grandchild may exhibit rage and ma-nipulative behaviours, refuse to do as you ask and act distant. She may also attach herself inappropriately to strangers or other adults, initiating an intimacy that is superficial. Be-

---

[3] These attachment strategies are from *Living with Prenatal Drug Exposure: A Guide for Parents* (2003), published by Groundwork Press and available at www.groundworkpress.com.

cause of her early experiences, your grandchild is unable to trust others, particularly those who are closest to her, like you. Attachment disorders can be very difficult to manage as, often, the children living with them are controlling, angry and dangerous to themselves and others. However, with consistent work, there are some attachment strategies that can help you parent your grandchild and help her to feel trust again. Remember that attachment issues are serious and complex; it is vital to seek help from your social worker, local family centre or therapist.

The following list offers some strategies for grandparents dealing with attachment.

STRATEGIES

Every difficult behaviour should be met with a **consequence**, no exceptions.

Remain calm, don't show any anger or irritation and respond to behaviour instead of reacting to it.

Don't let your grandchild control you with manipulating behaviours. Instead of reacting the way he expects or wants, surprise him with something completely unpredictable, such as reaching over and tickling him in the ribs when he is sulking.

Let your grandchild have an emotional, non-violent reaction when it's appropriate.

If he is out of control, put him in a room with the door firmly closed until he is able to behave calmly.

Maintain firm boundaries.

Give your grandchild the affection he may have missed as an infant.

If your grandchild resists touching, **establish what touches (pats on head, shaking hands) he is okay with** and work from there.

If your older grandchild or adolescent withdraws or expresses a desire to no longer be a part of the family, **find other ways of expressing your love** and commitment to him. For example, write notes or letters and place them where your grandchild can't miss them.

Make sure to **educate professionals** about attachment issues and strategies that work for your family. Expect that not everyone will understand and that some will blame your parenting techniques.

Get respite if you need it.

GRANDPARENTING SKILLS

We frequently wondered if we were going to really be able to do this and often felt like we were the only ones. But it did get easier, and we drew strength and hope from others who were doing what we were doing and discovered many grandparents facing much greater hurdles than we were, and doing it so successfully.

—Ralph and Barbara, caregiver grandparents

Becoming a parent[4] at any age is difficult. But taking on a child as you age comes with its own set of challenges. Although you're never too old to parent, the truth is that, as grandparents, you have less energy and mobility than you used to. Also, many children in these situations have complicated relationships with their parents, oftentimes carrying with them a weighty history of abuse or neglect. Building a healthy relationship with your grandchild that is based on love and respect is definitely doable, but not always easy. Often, raising a child comes in stages. Your grandchildren might be dropped off for one day, and then one week, until, before you know it, it's permanent.

The arrival of children in your home is very disruptive to your already set routine. Suddenly, your days are filled with diapers, bag lunches and getting the kids to school. Instead of enjoying your retirement, you find that you can't even stop to hear yourself think, let alone fill your days with leisurely pursuits. While many of your friends are enjoying simply being indulgent grandparents, you are weathering the stresses of being a primary caregiver.

There are a couple of big reasons why grandparents take on the raising of their grandchildren. One is that they're afraid the children will go into government care. The other

---

[4] Some of the information in this section is taken from *Adoption Piece by Piece: Lifelong Issues* (2003), published by Groundwork Press. Copies of this book are available at www.groundworkpress.com.

reason is simply because the children need to be cared for, and grandparents see no choice but to step up to the plate. Perhaps you've had a positive grandchild-grandparent relationship in which your grandchild counts on you for support and advice. Perhaps you've lent a sympathetic ear or a shoulder to cry on when life became tough for them.

In many cultures grandparents are the family members who communicate and keep alive traditions, ceremonies and beliefs. They are expected to pass on coping skills and experience in order to prepare children for adulthood. Yet, in spite of this, many youth still don't have close relationships with older adults. Sometimes this is due to the fact that the seniors in their families have passed on or live in another city. The importance of having positive role models who are older can help tremendously with a child's healthy growth and development. As someone who is parenting again after your children have grown, you have a chance to make an important and positive contribution to their upbringing.

It could be that, because you haven't raised children in a long time, you forget some things about being a parent. Brushing up on your parenting skills might seem strange for someone who has raised one child or more. But parenting has changed a lot from the child-rearing you might have done 20 or 30 years ago, just as the society around you has changed. Through TV and the Internet children are exposed to much more sex and violence than previous generations. You may find that you need to catch up on the ways children are growing up now, and the social influences around them, like the media. In addition, if your grandson or granddaughter comes from a drug-using or abusive home, he or she has already been forced to contend with adult issues before they're ready. Your grandchild may present challenging behaviours caused by the trauma they've experienced, or exhibit other behaviours typical of special needs conditions such as Fetal Alcohol Spectrum Disorder, Attention Deficit Disorder or Oppositional Defiant Disorder, to name a few.

Meanwhile, parenting philosophies have changed in recent years, particularly with regards to discipline. Physical punishment is generally no longer acceptable, and in some cases could be considered abusive, and might even be grounds for removing the child from your home. You may have forgotten over the years how children behave, and be out of touch with what acceptable behaviour is, and what can be modified. It is helpful to take a class to bring you up to speed on new parenting techniques that will teach you how to help children learn responsibility, accountability, confidence and self-esteem.

Parenting 101
Check out what's available at your local community centre, family service agency, library, neighbourhood house, community college or hospital. You'll be surprised to discover that many parenting classes are subsidized. This means that either they're free or that the cost is on the low end of the scale (i.e. $15 or less). Parenting classes go from infancy to teenage years and explore various kinds of parent stress such as behaviour issues and communicating with teens. Some classes discuss topics such as how to build healthy relationships with

your grandchildren or tips to help stay connected and enhance the child's self-esteem. Look into infant or toddler child development courses. Also pay a visit to your local library for a selection of books, videos and magazines that are available to help you out.

The information below should be used as a guide only as all children develop at different stages and respond to different techniques. If you're concerned with your grandchild's development it's a good idea to contact your family doctor or healthcare professional.

STRATEGIES

Infants
Chat with and listen to your grandbaby.

Play with her and make the communication game fun for both her and you.

As soon as she can manage a toy on her own, let her do so as this will **foster self-reliance and confidence**.

Give her **different toys and activities** to stimulate her.

Show her praise as she tries things on her own and learns from them.

Toddlers
Give praise and positive feedback such as "Well done" or "Good for you."

Tell your grandchild that **it's OK to make mistakes**.

Listen carefully to him, repeating what he said to make certain you've understood.

Teach him nursery rhymes and have conversations with him.

Help your grandchild express feelings such as "I'm upset because…" or "I feel happy when…."

Criticize behaviour, not your grandchild as you don't want him to think he's a bad person. For instance, if he is jumping up and down and crying because he can't watch his favourite program, instead of saying something like "Only bad boys jump up and down," try saying "I don't understand what it is you want to say. Please tell me what the matter is." This is very important as most behaviours can be modified. This is something you can both work toward together.

Mealtimes are the messiest as your toddler grandchild learns how to use a spoon and drink from a cup. By four years old there will be less to clean up as he'll be able to hold a cup and use a spoon and fork.

Focus on what your grandchild does well. This might be holding his cup or asking to go to the bathroom.

Don't focus on his failures. Instead, focus on the positives such as his ability to put on his shoes and jacket.

At this age and older the child might be afraid to sleep on his own. This could be related to a time when he was alone and felt unsafe. It could be that, when the lights go out, he relives past trauma related to abuse.

Keep a **nightlight** by his bed.

To help the child settle before bedtime it can be good to **have a set routine**: he has a bath, then you read him a story and, finally, you talk to him about what he's going to do tomorrow.

Maybe he has a **favourite stuffed toy** or blanket that makes him feel secure while he sleeps.

It might help him settle to **rub his back and sing** to him.

School Age

This time can be both exciting and stressful for your grandchild. Already by this young age she has probably been moved around once, twice or even more. Now, she is going off to school for the first time. Depending on what past trauma she has been through, this can be an emotionally trying time. That is why, even though she may not seem like she needs you, it's important to show her constant love and reassurance.

Tell her you will be there to pick her up after school.

Gradually introduce her to her new classroom and teachers

Mention a special activity you have planned for just the two of you on the weekend. Thinking of this will help her feel secure.

Have set times for meals and homework.

Keep reviewing rules throughout your grandchild's growth and development, changing them as she grows more competent.

Be careful about what words you choose. Instead of saying "You're so clumsy" or "Don't be stupid," try instead, "I see you tripped; are you OK?" Or, "Would you like me to help you with that?"

Give praise when called for, such as: "I see you picked up your books. Good for you." Or, "I like the way you made your bed without being asked."

When grandparents feel they have little or no control over a grandchild's behaviour they might decide that severe discipline is the way to go. But this tactic can backfire as it will cause the child to become angrier and act out.

Some disorders can cause children's behaviours to change. Talk to a healthcare provider so that they can assess your grandchild. Many disorders are easy to manage when you know about them earlier rather than later. Yet the type of special needs a child has will have an impact on how you manage their behaviours. For instance, a child with FASD may require more structure and routines, while a child with autism might take everything you say literally.

It's important to see a counsellor if your grandchild exhibits or has experienced any of the following:

- Abuse
- Depression
- Behavioural, psychological, emotional and medical concerns
- Extreme fear or anger
- Acting out sexually
- Cruelty to animals or others
- Bed-wetting
- Fire-setting
- Self-destructive tendencies
- Wanting to die

The child may be angry with you and perceive that you have sent her parents away; this could cause acting out. It could be that the child is used to insults and name-calling so is very sensitive about it.

Never tease or ridicule the child, or partake in swearing or shouting.

Instead of *losing your cool* with your grandchild, it's better to help her **direct her anger** by expressing herself through words that you can then validate as you listen.

If the child is unable to express verbally what is the matter, then **give her a pillow to punch** in order to work it out physically.

Through your good examples, you'll teach your grandchild that **swearing or insulting or hitting someone you love isn't respectful** and love is about respect. These are lessons that she will carry with her throughout her lifetime.

Teens

Grandparents can often feel that the child has been through enough upset and that any discipline at all will only harm him. Yet all children—even teens—require clear rules and expectations. Research shows that parents who are more involved in this way are more likely to have solid, healthy relationships than parents who allow their children to do as they wish without limits. For grandparents, the challenge is that you may still be hanging on to the indulgent grandchild-grandparent relationship. This relationship may have included buying treats and special gifts for the grandchild. While there is nothing wrong with this, you may find you need to establish a different relationship with your grandchild based on these new and difficult circumstances. Having your grandchild live with you full-time, or much of the time, means added responsibility, which comes with being the primary caregiver. Instead of knitting that birthday sweater or buying a pair of hockey tickets for her, you might be putting money aside for an upcoming dental appointment or school supplies. While this might not be as fun to you or her, remember that providing for daily needs right now is the best possible gift.

Unlike before, you might find yourself assigning weekly chores to your teen grandchild such as making her bed or watering the plants. It's important to be aware of where your grandchild is and how she's doing in school. In addition, setting a curfew is all part of raising a teenager who learns to respect you and her own self in turn.

Due to past trauma related to abuse or neglect, a teen might be labelled at-risk. Understanding why the teen needs extra support will help you determine when to ask for help either from a friend or professional before a difficult situation escalates. Some of the common behaviours of at-risk teens involve the following:

- Discipline problems such as acting out in class
- Problems going to the next grade
- Lack of confidence
- Bullying peers
- Drug or alcohol use.

Lend a sympathetic ear by listening to your grandchild's concerns and fears. Encourage him to be involved in school activities and community events and provide a home environment that is comfortable and nurturing.

Discipline Techniques

Discipline is a big challenge for parents, but for grandparents it represents additional challenges. You might previously have been a *buddy* to your grandchild with little time spent disciplining him, and now find yourself in the role of parent. You might not wish to undermine your adult child's authority by disciplining, as, after all, she is the child's biological parent. However, until the time your grandchild goes back to live with his family—if in fact that ever happens—you are the child's primary caregiver. Your grandchild will test your limits and might exhibit some behaviours that will test your patience as well! That's why, even if the child does eventually return to his parents, you'll need to have a few techniques up your sleeve to make sure that his stay with you is positive and instructive for both of you.

Another challenge for grandparents parenting a second time is that grandchildren whose parents are in difficulty—with drugs, alcohol or something else—very often deal with challenging behaviours related to specific challenges. If, for instance you find out that your grandchild is affected by FASD as a result of her mother's alcohol addiction, or is diagnosed with attachment disorder due to neglect, then this must be considered when researching discipline techniques that work. For information on possible challenges, please see Chapter 4 in Part 2: Special Needs.

As you've already learned in this chapter, discipline techniques have dramatically changed from the time you were a parent. The philosophy has shifted its focus to building on a child's abilities rather than always pointing out what he does wrong. This different approach increases self-esteem and helps diffuse negative behaviours. Contrary to punishment, discipline helps children learn self-control, gain confidence and care about others as well as themselves. Here are some ways to help you with disciplining your grandchild.

Time-out

When a child acts out, direct her to a place such as a separate room or chair so she can be alone and have some space to calm down. You might start this by saying "You need a time out." Time-outs will vary in length based on the child and situation. You might wish to set a kitchen timer to two minutes and then go and see whether the child has calmed down enough to talk about the reasons behind her behaviours.

Consequences

This form of discipline teaches the child that there are outcomes attached to her actions. If the child breaks a toy, instead of buying another one to replace it, explain to the child that the toy is permanently gone now because it is broken. Sometimes children don't understand why a child won't play with them due to a challenging behaviour she has exhibited. In such a situation, explain to the child why the other child doesn't want to play with her and suggest that, next time, she share her toys or not hit the other child. Just as there are consequences for negative behaviour, there are also consequences for positive ones as well. If your grandchild has helped you set the table or make dinner, you can let her know that this gives you more time to help her with homework or to watch a favourite show with her.

Redirect

When your grandchild is about to do something he isn't supposed to, redirect the child's attention to something he's allowed to do. For example, if he is starting to play with a breakable object, show him a favourite toy and suggest he play with that instead.

Ignore

Some children misbehave just to get attention. Reacting every time this occurs can not only be exhausting, but is usually counter-productive to teaching the child correct behaviour. Instead, try giving your grandchild positive attention when she behaves well. If you only pay attention to her and react when she exhibits a negative behaviour then she will continue to act out, as she getting what she desires, which is your undivided attention.

It Takes a Community

You've probably heard of the expression: "It takes a community to raise a child." Well, this is true whether you're a parent raising your biological or adoptive child or a grandparent having another go-around at being a parent. Surrounding yourself with a supportive team of people—family members and friends who are willing to play an active role in your grandchild's life—is the best recipe for success. Make certain that these are caring people who know and understand your grandchild and how to deal with his or her behaviour; in other words, people with whom the child feels comfortable. What about assigning specific activities to these people so that, for instance, your son or daughter counts on them to watch a movie every second Friday evening or help with math homework? Or, what about finding a younger role model that the child can do more active stuff with such as play Frisbee or softball. If you don't have anyone in mind you could always try a community organization such as Big Brothers or Big Sisters, or, if you attend church, contact the youth pastor to see what programs for young people are available. Above all, don't isolate yourself. Connect with others and seek counselling as required. Join a support group for grandparents. Supporting yourself is the best support you can give your grandchild.

Family Dynamics

Depending on the situation, your child might still have regular contact with your adult child. For legal guardians, your guardianship order may include visitation rights. On-going contact between the children and parents can be extremely positive if boundaries and expectations are clear, and if the parents are fit or safe to be in the child's life. However, if your son or daughter is still struggling with addictions or other problems, these visits can be very stressful for both you and your grandchildren. If this is the case it's best to have outside support so you can air your concerns and perhaps re-negotiate visitation ground rules as needed.

The child may be afraid that she will have to leave you if her parents come back. Or she may fear that her parents will never come back for her. Adult children may promise to do things that they don't deliver on. They might think they will parent again and tell their children that, only to break that promise. In this situation, a child will experience grief and loss for a parent who keeps coming and going. During this time, reassure your grandchild that you will not leave her and that she is safe. For more on grief and loss in grandchildren, please see Chapter 2 in Part 2: Your Grandchild's Emotions. If your adult child is still battling issues such as drug or alcohol abuse and you are worried about the child being taken away from you, document facts relating to visits with parents, along with expenses that show how much you are contributing to the child's daily expenses. This will help greatly in case of legal proceedings. More detail on legal issues is included in Chapter 5 in Part 2: Systems.

SPECIAL NEEDS

We try to channel our grandson's energy in positive ways, and give lots of positive reinforcement, but it's difficult when he is being cruel to his sister or getting in difficulty with classmates.

—Ralph and Barbara, caregiver grandparents

The term *special needs*[5] can mean a variety of things. It most commonly refers to a special condition or disability affecting the child, be it medical (e.g. FASD, malnutrition, etc.), physical (e.g. cerebral palsy, spina bifida, etc.), emotional and behavioural (e.g. attachment disorder, conduct disorder, etc.), or historical (e.g., history of abuse and neglect, multiple foster home placements, etc.). Special needs can also refer to unique living situations, such as children whose parents have passed away. Or children, like yours, who are living with their grandparents.

In terms of specific special needs, there is a wide range of conditions you might encounter with your grandchild, from Fragile X Syndrome to Fetal Alcohol Spectrum Disorder (FASD). Obviously, it is impossible for us to address all of these in one chapter. But in the following sections we will touch on some of the most prevalent special needs conditions you might encounter: invisible disabilities including learning disabilities, FASD, Neonatal Abstinence Syndrome (NAS)/prenatal drug exposure (PDE), attachment issues, Attention Deficit Disorder with and without hyperactivity (ADD/ADHD), Conduct Disorder, and history of abuse and neglect. In Part 3: Workbook, we have included a development table and assessment checklist for your use when monitoring your grandchild's progress. Re-

---

[5] Much of the information in this section is taken from *Adoption Piece by Piece: Special Needs* (2003) and *Living with Prenatal Drug Exposure: A Guide for Parents* (2003), published by Groundwork Press. Copies are available at www.groundworkpress.com. Additional information is from Groundwork Press' parent organization SNAP (www.snap.bc.ca).

member that these are brief outlines only and that, for more detail and treatment options, we encourage grandparents to talk to their family doctor, pediatrician or special education teacher. If you feel that the professional you're talking to does not believe or is dismissing your concerns, then seek out a second opinion. Often your instincts will point you in the right direction.

A special note to grandparents whose grandchild has *other* special needs not on this list: if the condition you're facing isn't named or discussed here, it doesn't mean that it's less important, or that it doesn't have a significant impact on your family. It may simply be less common, that's all. We encourage you to find all the information you can about your child's particular special needs. Educate yourself, the professionals in your child's life, and the public at large. Your local community centre or family association is a great place to start as they often have resource libraries and people there to help you find what you're looking for.

Some Common Conditions

Asperger Syndrome

The term Asperger syndrome comes from Hans Asperger who, in 1944, linked the condition to autism. Individuals with Asperger often find it difficult to interpret information and may take things that are said to them literally. Because they don't easily pick up on social signals, sufferers of the syndrome often have difficulty communicating with their peers and feel socially isolated. They can become preoccupied with subjects typically of interest to children older than themselves. Although they aren't always able to communicate, these individuals typically possess good verbal skills and are of average intelligence.

Though there is no treatment or cure for the disorder, early intervention in the form of one-on-one counselling, parent education training, and behavioural modification goes a long way to helping combat difficulties associated with social interaction and creating lasting relationships. Contrary to lower functioning autism, individuals with Asperger Syndrome function at a higher level. They often experience less severe social and communication breakdowns. Also, their verbal IQ is usually higher than performance IQ, whereas in autism it is usually the opposite. The cause of Asperger is not yet known, however current research suggests that varying forms of this condition may run in families.

Attachment and Bonding

Bonding is the unique relationship between a child and caregiver that occurs as a result of physical proximity during pregnancy, childbirth and/or early childhood. *Attachment* is a long-lasting psychological and emotional connectedness between human beings.

When a child suffers trauma, be it through neglect or abuse, he has difficulty bonding or attaching to a caregiver. The normal development he must go through is impeded, causing the child to develop a sense of mistrust, internalized rage and a need to control situations. It is important to help the child develop a trusting relationship with others, most of all with his caregivers. If this is not done the child won't be able to form any long-lasting relationships with others. Some therapies to assist the child in attaching to the caregiver include regressive therapy, behaviour management, and re-parenting.

Reactive Attachment Disorder (RAD) refers to a specific attachment disorder associated with neglectful, abusive or inconsistent care. It is characterized by inappropriate social behaviour such as unresponsiveness or indiscriminate affection, a need for control, anger and defiance. Due to a deep mistrust of adults, the child often has a need to resist the caregiver. The child may try to push her caregiver away with an unwillingness to show affection. She may also act out or form inappropriately close relationships with strangers.

Attention Deficit Disorder (ADD)/Attention Hyperactivity Disorder (ADHD)
Note: These two definitions exist because not all children with ADD are hyperactive.

Roughly 5-10% of all children exhibit some form of ADD/ADHD, with 20% of these displaying a severe form. Both disorders frequently come with learning disabilities. Although ADD/ADHD does not affect intelligence and is not related to mental retardation, intellectual development is often inconsistent. For instance, the child may be ahead in math and behind in reading. It is thought that these disorders are caused by chemical differences in the brain that may be linked to inborn temperamental differences. These disorders are characterized by being easily distracted, short attention span, fidgeting, talking without stopping, and difficulty concentrating. Children with ADD/ADHD often have trouble controlling their impulses. They may become upset when things or people fail to behave as they should. These children often have mood swings which means they may be happy one minute and sad the next. For this reason, their behaviour is unpredictable. Medications most frequently used to treat these conditions are stimulant drugs such as d-amphetamine (e.g. Dexedrine) and methylphenidate (e.g. Ritalin). However, some children do not respond well to medication and may need other kinds of treatment such as behavioural interventions.

There are many approaches to raising a child who has ADD. One way might be to establish a consistent set of rules, always with the same set of consequences. If the child breaks the rules, it is important that he be disciplined in some way in order to learn. There are many approaches to providing for the needs of a child who has ADD. As each case is unique, it is important to try different methods to see what suits the specific child.

Autism
Autism is one of the most common developmental disabilities. It is a brain disorder that affects an individual's ability to communicate, interact with others and respond to his or her surroundings. Some people with autism have a relatively high intelligence level whereas others may be developmentally delayed or have serious language delays. Autism

is not caused by faulty parenting, abuse, neglect or childhood trauma. There is no known cause of autism and as yet there is no cure. Through early diagnosis, children can benefit from intervention techniques that modify behaviour by using positive reinforcement for appropriate behaviours. Applied Behavioural Analysis (ABA), medication, and nutrition have all proved helpful in treating autism.

Bi-polar disorder

Another name for bi-polar disorder is manic depression. It is a mood disorder character-ized by extreme mood shifts, depressive lows—during which the person will experience symptoms of depression such as sleeping all the time, lack of energy and feelings of de-spair—and manic highs, which are periods when the individual will be uncharacteristically cheerful, have difficulty concentrating on one task at a time and sleep very little. Thoughts of suicide are also common.

Children and adolescents can be diagnosed with bi-polar disorder. In children, periods of depression and mania can occur several times in a day, whereas adults will often experience more sustained cycles, over several days or even weeks. Symptoms in adolescents are more similar to adult symptoms. As well, bi-polar disorder in children can be very difficult to identify as symptoms can be attributed to other conditions like ADHD or Conduct Disorder.

Conduct Disorder (CD)

The main difference between Conduct Disorder and Oppositional Defiant Disorder (ODD) is that a child with CD will often consistently violate the rights or comfort of others and/or major social rules. This means that the safety of the child as well as the safety of his or her family and community may be at risk through theft, deceitfulness, violence or destruction of property. The child also typically displays a lack of empathy. Conduct Disorder may grow out of Oppositional Defiant Disorder and, like ODD, can be treated with behaviour modi-fication. It also often appears in combination with other disorders which makes treatment more complex. It is important to note that some children who come from disadvantaged communities where Conduct Disorder-like behaviour is part of daily survival may not actually have the disorder itself.

Down's syndrome

Down's syndrome is the most common form of severe mental retardation. In North America, Down's syndrome occurs for one in one thousand births. Parents do not cause Down's syndrome. A child with Down's syndrome has one extra chromosome on each of his or her millions of cells. Because their characteristic appearance is easily recognizable, there is a tendency to see them as all the same. However, each Down's syndrome child has his or her own unique personality.

Dyslexia

Dyslexia comes from 'dys' meaning trouble and 'lex' meaning words. 20% of the population is affected by dyslexia at a male-female ratio of 4-1. Dyslexia sometimes shows up in reading, handwriting and spelling, and in organizing spoken and written information. Dyslexic students often have trouble in school and are sometimes thought to be developmentally handicapped, uncooperative and lazy. Often, letters or numerals are reversed and letters or syllables are read and written in a confused order. Multi-sensory training in school has proven effective in teaching dyslexic students to read and write. This technique uses visual, auditory, kinesthetic (movement) and tactile prompts.

Fetal Alcohol Spectrum Disorder (FASD)

Fetal Alcohol Spectrum Disorder is an umbrella term that encompasses all the conditions related to prenatal alcohol exposure. This includes Fetal Alcohol Syndrome (FAS), Partial Fetal Alcohol Syndrome (pFAS) and Alcohol Related Neurodevelopmental Disorder (ARND).

Fetal Alcohol Syndrome was first defined over thirty years ago. It is an organic brain disorder that refers to a set of physical and mental birth defects a child may develop as a result of his or her mother consuming alcohol during pregnancy. It is characterized by central nervous system involvement, growth retardation and characteristic facial features. A medical diagnosis can only be made when a child has signs of abnormalities in each of these three areas as well as known FAS or suspected exposure to alcohol prenatally. FAS is also associated with a number of secondary characteristics such as poor judgement, an inability to process information and form causal links, impulsivity, a tendency to be easily influenced and superficial verbal fluency. FAS is often classed as a *hidden* or *invisible* disability because its physical characteristics often go undetected.

Partial Fetal Alcohol Syndrome, which is also known as Fetal Alcohol Effects (FAE), applies to a person with a confirmed history of prenatal alcohol exposure who has some, but not all, of the characteristics of FAS. This does not mean, however, that pFAS is any less severe; it can have serious implications for education, social functioning and vocational success.

Alcohol Related Neurodevelopmental Disorder differs from both FAS and pFAS in that there are few or no characteristic facial features. Individuals with ARND often have normal or above average intelligence as well as some secondary characteristics that are associated with FAS.

Information on FASD and its related conditions can be found in Groundwork Press' bestselling book, *Living with FASD: A Guide for Parents* (2003), available at www.groundworkpress.com.

Learning Disabilities

This is a general term referring to a group of disorders due to identifiable or interred central nervous system dysfunction. Such disorders may be manifested by delays of early development and or difficulties in any of the following areas: attention, memory, reasoning, coordination, communicating, reading, writing, spelling, calculations, social competence and emotional maturity.

Neonatal Abstinence Syndrome (NAS)
This is a condition affecting children exposed to opiate drugs before birth. Infants with NAS go through withdrawal after birth because of dependency causing substances such as heroin and methadone taken by the mother during pregnancy. Symptoms of NAS may be present at the infant's birth or may not begin until several days after delivery depending on the drug or drugs taken by the mother. Withdrawal can take as little as three weeks or as long as six months. There is little known about the long term effects of exposure to some drugs that may result in NAS.

Oppositional Defiant Disorder (ODD)
ODD is a psychiatric disorder that begins to appear around one to three years of age. The most prominent characteristics of the disorder are aggression and a persistent desire to upset others. A child with ODD will often argue with and defy adults, blame others for his/her mistakes or misbehaviour and be resentful and easily annoyed. ODD often occurs in combination with other disorders such as ADHD or depression and anxiety; as well, it may develop into Conduct Disorder as the child grows older. Some children will respond to consistent behaviour modification.

Prenatal Drug Exposure (PDE)
This term refers to a spectrum of conditions that may result from exposure to drugs before birth, including opiates, stimulants and prescription drugs. It is not a diagnostic term in itself. A range of drugs such as cocaine, heroin, methadone, Talwin, Ritalin, Codeine, marijuana, inhalants, and Valium affects children. Whereas the term prenatal drug exposure is not drug specific, NAS is a specific diagnosis applied to newborns who are withdrawing from intrauterine exposure to opiates. The term PDE also comprises alcohol exposure before birth. However, because a pregnant mother's alcohol consumption can result in conditions that are part of Fetal Alcohol Spectrum Disorder (FASD) with their own set of distinctive manifestations and challenges, PDE is most often used to refer to drug exposure alone. Researchers have yet to explore in depth the extent to which prenatal substance exposure affects behavioural development. The impact on a child of an unstable home environment, and poor pre- and post-natal nutrition and care make it difficult to link behaviours to drugs alone.

Psychological and Emotional Abuse

Psychology comes from the Greek words *psyche* meaning the mind, soul or spirit, and *logos* meaning discourse or study. Children as young as two months old can be victims of psychological abuse. This type of abuse in children scars by recurring, inappropriate emotional responses by caregivers in the form of aggression, indifference, rejection and terror. These responses reduce the creative and developmental potential of a child's mental faculties and processes, which include intelligence, memory and recognition, perceptions, attention, language and moral development.

Humans are born with the capacity to feel and express emotion. Expressing emotion is a vital part of a child's development. The caregiver's emotional response will determine how well the child bonds and his or her level of attachment. Hindering a child's emotions through emotional abuse can significantly harm his or her emotional growth.

Schizophrenia

This is a mental disorder marked by a difficulty to distinguish between what is real and what is imagined. People with this disorder often have difficulty holding down a job, interacting with others and going to school. As yet there is no cure for schizophrenia. It is important to remember that schizophrenia is not the fault of poor parenting. People with schizophrenia have a chemical imbalance. It is thought that the brain may produce too much of a chemical called dopamine, a neurotransmitter allowing nerve cells in the brain to send messages to each other. People with schizophrenia process sounds, sights, smells and tastes in a different way. This can lead to hallucinations or delusions. Often the disease runs in families. It can surface when the body undergoes hormonal and physical changes like those occurring during puberty. It may also be caused by viral infections or highly stressful events.

Sexual Abuse

The definition of the National Center of Child Abuse and Neglect reads "sexual abuse consists of contacts or interactions between a child and an adult when the child is being used for the sexual stimulation of that adult or of another person."

Tourette Syndrome (TS)

This is a physical disorder which causes uncontrollable movements (known as motor tics) and vocal sounds (known as vocal tics). Tourette syndrome is often characterized by hyperactivity and impulsive and volatile behaviour. Depending on the severity, these motor tics include eye blinking, grimacing, shrugging, hand jerking and head movements. Vocal tics can include grunts, shouts, repeated phrases and obscenity laced speech. Medications exist to treat TS symptoms; however, the first step is to educate the people in the child's environment (teachers, parents of peers, etc.) so that appropriate modifications can be made that may circumvent the need for medication.

When You Don't Have a Diagnosis

It is perfectly understandable for the caregiver grandparent to want to have a diagnosis for his or her grandchild that is clear-cut and doesn't diverge into other areas of diagnosis. The complex nature of multiple special needs or developmental disabilities sometimes means that grandparents may feel frustration and loss at realizing that a simple diagnosis isn't probable. Deciding to focus on a child's strengths and working on challenging and ever-changing behaviours and characteristics is a way to positively influence a child's future. Talk to your family doctor or a specialist about positive activities or exercises designed for your grandchild's specific needs that you can implement to help with her development, even without a diagnosis. Remember too that your child's challenges are a part of her, in the same way that her brown eyes and musical talent are parts of her. While it is hard not to feel anger or sadness at her particular condition or disability, it is a good idea to accept it as one of your grandchild's characteristics, but not her defining one.

SYSTEMS

I am now 70 years old and all my savings are gone. I have had to sell the house I loved in an area I loved in order to scale down. My grandson is eating into my pension and I cannot wait for him to be grown up so that maybe at the end of the month I would have a plus balance instead of having to worry all the time.

—Ina, caregiver grandparent

As a grandparent caregiver, you may find yourself dealing with legal, medical and educational systems that are often confusing. These systems very rarely take into consideration the existence of custodial grandparents and you may experience a great deal of difficulty trying to obtain the services, support or resources you need. Knowing exactly what is available to you is the first step in advocating effectively for your family.

The Legal System

The legal system is often the first thing you encounter when you take on the task of parenting your grandchildren. Perhaps your grandchild came into your home because he or she was apprehended by child welfare workers. Perhaps you're living with your grandchild voluntarily, and are wondering where you stand in the system and how you can get help with your expenses. Or, perhaps you're parenting your grandchild completely under the radar and are afraid that your adult child, who still has legal custody and full parental rights, will one day arrive at your door and take your grandchild away.

The following is a brief outline of custody options available to most Canadian grandparents. However, please note that kinship care options vary from province to province, so please check with your local child protection office (look in the blue pages of your local phone book or check your provincial government's website) or consult with a family lawyer to see what is available. There may be programs available to you that are not included here. This section is not intended as legal advice, and we encourage all grandparents to consult a lawyer or call their local free law helpline.

In-care Placements

In-care placements are arrangements that involve your local child welfare authority. What this means is that the custody of your grandchild is with the government, who acts as the legal guardian. The caregiver grandparent is usually designated as a foster parent (for example in BC, your home would be called a "restricted foster home"), with compensation close to or equal to the payments that regular foster parents would receive, including coverage for dental and optical expenses. Other supports, like respite and counselling, may also be available.

Many grandparents come to foster their grandchildren because of child protection issues. Perhaps your adult child was abusing or neglecting your grandchildren. Usually, social workers have removed the grandchild from his or her home and then ask you to act as a foster parent in order to limit the disruption and emotional turmoil your grandchild feels. Sometimes, the parent has asked the child protection authority to become involved, and has voluntarily agreed to placing the child in government care. As a foster parent, you must submit to a criminal record check and home study.

Although this option provides a level of compensation and other supports that make daily life a little easier for grandparents who are worried about expenses and therapies, some grandparents do not like the idea of being a foster parent. Plans in the best interest of your grandchild are made by social workers because the government has legal custody. As a result, you may feel that your social worker is watching your every move, and that your authority is undermined by the regulations of your provincial government. As well, it may be that your grandchild will be removed from your home if your social worker thinks that a better home could be found. Many grandparents worry over their age and health, and fear that the child protection agencies will think that they will soon be unable to care for their grandchildren. Also, you may feel that your parenting skills are under suspicion because of the way your adult child turned out. You may wonder if your social worker is asking herself, "Well, if they didn't do such a good job with their own child, what makes them think they can do a better one with their grandchild?"

Remember as well that the goal for foster care is usually the return of the child to his or her parents. You may support this, hoping that your adult child gets her life organized enough that she will be able to take the child back into her home. On the other hand, this may fill you with fear if you feel that your adult child will likely never be able to parent again because of mental illness, drug addiction or other reasons.

There is also the possibility that your adult child's parental rights will be relinquished or taken away, and your grandchild may become available for adoption. While you can apply to adopt your grandchild yourself, you may fear that adoption social workers will not look favourably on your application because of age, health, finances or another reason.

However, many grandparents who are designated as foster parents find that this is the best option. If you're feeling low or at the end of your rope, you can access many services to help you through a rough patch. Because your family has been assigned a social worker whose responsibility is to ensure the health and happiness of your grandchild, you are never alone in parenting. If your grandchild is in need of counselling or specialized equipment for a disability, you will be able to obtain it. And, everyday costs like groceries and clothing are covered by the payments you receive from the government.

Out-of-care Options

Out-of-care means that the care of your grandchild has never officially been under the supervision of your local child welfare authority. There are several different ways this can happen.

Your arrangement with your adult child may be entirely private. This means that the legal custody of your grandchild is still with her parents and that you are an interim caregiver. Your family has never been involved with child protection workers (although this does not mean that your grandchild has not experienced abuse or neglect, just that it has never come to the attention of the child welfare office). In BC, grandparents who are living with their grandchildren without the presence of the children's parents can apply for funding from the Child in the Home of a Relative (CIHR) program administered by the Ministry of Employment and Income Assistance (MEIA). In Ontario, grandparents can apply to the Temporary Care program managed by Ontario Works. Payments are based on the child's income and assets, meaning that the more money your grandchild has, usually investments passed on to him from his parents, the smaller the payment. Some other provinces also provide some form of financial assistance to private arrangements, so check with your local child welfare office. Also, if your family is Aboriginal, you may be eligible for programs administered by your band or Indian and Northern Affairs Canada.

A social worker, alerted to a child protection issue in your grandchild's home, may have helped arrange your parenting situation. In many provinces, child protection workers will search for an alternative to foster care, often going to relatives first. If this is the case, you may have some kind of kinship care agreement (in BC, this is called a Kith and Kin Agreement) that is usually an agreement between the relative, in this case, a grandparent, the parent and the social worker that passes on care of the child to the relative. This kind of arrangement, like an informal one, does not come under the supervision of the child welfare office or foster care program, although a social worker may, from time to time, check up on your family. Financial support of the grandchild is usually up to the grandparent (although you may be eligible for some programs, such as Temporary Care in Ontario and the national Canada Child Tax Benefit) and other benefits, like respite and dental care is only available in exceptional circumstances. Most Canadian provinces offer no compensation under these agreements, although some money is available in BC if negotiated at the time of agreement development, and in the Calgary area, where a pilot kinship care program is currently being operated.

Permanent custody
Grandparents have two permanency options available to them. One is the permanent transfer of custody, which makes you the legal guardian of your grandchild. This arrangement can be formalized by a written agreement between the grandparents and parents of the child or through a court order if there is a child protection issue. Like any legal document, this written agreement can specify conditions particular to the situation, such as visitation with the parents or financial support, and provide for a review of the custody arrangement at some future date. Transfer of custody is a more permanent option than foster care, kinship care or informal care. Financial assistance is available based on need, but in general, the financial support of your grandchild is your responsibility. You may be subject to a criminal record and references check, as well as an assessment of your relationship with your grandchild. Your grandchild may also be interviewed to determine her views on this custody application.

Second, you could apply to adopt your grandchild. Your adult child's parental rights would have to be relinquished or taken away before this can happen; your adult child may even voluntarily enter into an adoption. An adoption is permanent and you would be named your grandchild's parent; all financial support is your responsibility, although some assistance may be available if your grandchild has special needs that require certain therapies or equipment. Like all potential adoptive parents, you would be subject to a full home study and background checks before the adoption can be approved. While ongoing supports are rarely available after an adoption has been made legal (check with your local adoption association or society to see what services you can still access), the advantage is that you will no longer have custody concerns. Your grandchild will always remain in your care.

Access
In BC, grandparents are protected by law through the amended Family Relations Act if one or both of your grandchild's parents decide to keep your grandchild from spending time or visiting you. This most often happens during a divorce, when the parent who has custody tries to keep the child away from the other parent (your adult child) and his or her family. In the BC courts, the grandparents are taken into account when determining what is in the best interest of the child.

Other provinces may not have any laws or amendments that protect the rights of grandparents when determining access. In that case, you can try mediation or even go to court to gain access to your grandchildren, but it is best to try and work these issues out within the family. There is no guarantee that a judge or mediator will recommend access in your favour (your adult child and/or his partner may exaggerate or even lie to keep you away). Be persistent. Ask your grandchild's parents to sit down and have a calm discussion with you to talk about why they do not want you in their child's life. Refrain from judging them or their parenting methods; after all, the goal is for you to spend time with your grandchild and arguing with the parents will not help. Write a letter if they refuse to see you or talk to you on the phone. Emphasize how much you miss the grandchild and suggest that the grandchild must miss you as well. As a last resort, consult a family lawyer to find out what your options are.

If you are caring for your grandchild and you have been attending visits with your adult child, you may find that these visits disturb or upset your grandchild for a variety of reasons. Perhaps your adult child is angry and perceives that you are turning your grandchild against her. Maybe she has a drug problem and acts erratically in front of you and your grandchild. Or perhaps she lifts your grandchild's hopes by promising that he will very soon come to live with her, even though she has made and broken the very same promise many times before.

If your grandchild was removed from his parents' home because of child protection issues and you are acting as a foster parent or have a kinship care agreement with the child welfare authority, talk to your social worker, who may be able to help you obtain a restraining order through the courts. If you have adopted your grandchild, then your adult child has relinquished her parental rights, and you do not have to allow a visit with your grandchild unless you want to, or unless you have an open adoption agreement (an agreement between the birth family and adoptive family that outlines the kind of contact the child and adoptive family has with the birth family). However, if your caregiving arrangement is a private one, and your adult child has maintained her parental rights, there isn't much you can do to prevent visits. Talk to a family lawyer or call your local free law helpline for information about possibly obtaining a restraining order. In order to obtain one, you will have to prove that your adult child's visits are harmful to your grandchild, so it's a good idea to keep a detailed record, including dates and times, of these visits, and write down what your adult child says and does, as well as her state of mind and the impact on your grandchild. While a judge may not deem this kind of journal admissible in court, it may still come in handy in mediation or other custody discussions.

Keeping the Finances in Order
Many grandparents find their financial lives in disarray when their grandchildren arrive and take up residence in their homes. Even if the families are receiving compensation from the

government, often this compensation falls short in varying ways, perhaps lacking coverage for dental care or for the start-up costs associated with taking a child into your home (necessities such as a child-safe bed, a high chair and baby gates to keep toddlers away from stairs). Because so many grandparents are retired and on fixed incomes this is a particularly pressing issue. This section will outline some things you can do to help with your childcare costs, although we strongly suggest contacting your local child welfare office, as well as a professional financial planner if you have the resources to access one.

Government Assistance

Depending on the custody arrangement you have with your grandchild, adult child and social worker, you may be eligible for a number of financial assistance programs. If you are caring for your child as a foster parent, you are entitled to foster care payments that are usually about $800 per month per child. Other benefits, like dental coverage, a child care subsidy (which, depending on the jurisdiction, pays for daycare or another kind of childcare), respite and support from a social worker for any parenting issues, are offered as well.

If you have an out-of-care arrangement, whether it is informally with your grandchild's parents, or facilitated through a social worker, you will receive much less, sometimes nothing. In BC, relatives who care for a child can apply to the CIHR program (see above) and receive up to $460 per month per child, depending on age and other factors. This is only available to grandparents who do not have a Kith and Kin Agreement. In Ontario, the Temporary Care program can pay up to $270 per month per child, depending on the child's assets and income (any more than $500 and your payments will go down). In Calgary through the Child and Family Services Authority, some grandparents may be eligible for kinship care payments, which are close to the payments foster homes receive. Some provinces offer some compensation and some offer nothing at all, stating that the care of family members should be the financial responsibility of the family, not of the government. Aboriginal agencies and bands may also provide some money from Indian and Northern Affairs Canada. Check with your local child welfare office to see what options are available to you.

Grandparents caring for their grandchildren can also apply for the Canada Child Tax Benefit, which can pay up to $270 per child per month. You will have to fill out the Canada Child Tax Benefit application form, available through the Canada Revenue Agency and its website at www.cra-arc.gc.ca.

If you are working and need to take time off when your grandchild first comes to live with you, you may be eligible for Employment Insurance (EI) benefits by claiming parental leave. This is worth about 55% of your employment income to a maximum of $413 per week. You can receive EI benefits for up to 45 weeks. Applications are available through your local Service Canada Centre or through the Human Resources and Social Development Canada website at www.hrsdc.gc.ca.

You can also claim your grandchild as a dependent on your income tax return and receive a tax credit of about $6,500 if you are a single caregiver. You can also claim childcare and some medical expenses (those that are not covered by your provincial health care program or insurance), but these write-offs are only available if you are still working. It's also possible to employ your grandchild and pay him a wage, thus further reducing your income tax payments. Keep in mind, however, that the salary you pay your grandchild has to be reasonable and that this is only a benefit if your grandchild's income is low enough that he doesn't have to pay extra taxes himself.

If you are classified as low income, you may also be eligible for subsidized housing in some cities. This is especially key for grandparents who find that they have to move because of space or apartment regulations when their grandchildren arrive. As well, in some cities, transit passes are available to low income seniors.

Financial Planning

Even if you're not eligible for any government programs, or you wish to not involve the government in the care of your grandchildren, there are several things you can do to ensure that you have enough income to cover additional costs. You may also want to plan for the future when you are one day unable to take as active a role in parenting your grandchild.

It is important for you to plan your finances with a lawyer, accountant or other financial advisor to explore all the options open to you. This kind of planning can become very complicated very quickly, and you want to work with someone who can explain every step to you.

FINANCIAL TIPS

If you own your own home, **you can apply for a reverse mortgage**, which turns the equity in your home into cash. Payments come monthly, so if you are retired and do not need to move, this is an option for obtaining some extra money. Talk to a financial planner to see if this will work for you.

You can **invest in RESPs** for the future education of your grandchild. Government top-ups to RESP contributions can amount to $400 per year per child. Plus, you receive tax benefits from your contributions and all earnings from interest are tax-free until the investment is cashed in.

Whole life insurance can also be a good investment as it can be cashed in with no restrictions (unlike a RESP). Premiums are generally very low for children under 18.

Invest in RRSPs for your grandchild as soon as he begins to earn an income. Like RESPs, the contributions can be claimed on your income tax return and the earnings are tax-free.

You can **set up a trust fund** of some kind for your grandchild that matures at an age you specify. It's wise to consult a financial advisor if this is something you are considering because of complicated income tax regulations.

Housing

When your grandchildren move in with you, you may find that your home is too small or not appropriate for your new family configuration. Perhaps you sold your house years ago and have downsized into a one-bedroom apartment. Or, perhaps you live in an adult-oriented complex that doesn't allow any children under the age of 18. Perhaps you would also like to find a home close to your grandchildren's familiar neighbourhood so that they don't have to change schools or find new friends.

Finding a new home that is both appropriate and affordable can be a very tough thing, especially if you are retired and are receiving little or no help from government programs. As we mentioned before, if you're lucky enough to own your home and are able to stay there with your grandchildren, a reverse mortgage can be a good idea. If this is not an option, look into government-subsidized housing (usually apartments or townhomes), sometimes available in your community for families with low incomes. Or, research cooperative housing, which means that a group of families each pay once into the co-op (usually in the range of $1,200 to $5,000) when they move in, and then have the advantage of paying much less than market rent for their units (like subsidized housing, usually apartments or townhomes), sometimes as little as 25 percent. The residents, as a collective, own the land and buildings of the co-op.

The Healthcare System[6]

After your grandchild comes to live with you, you will at some point need to take her to a doctor. Maybe the child will run a high temperature related to a flu bug that's going around. Or it could be that you suspect the child is affected by FASD. Even a healthy grandchild needs regular check-ups and immunizations. If possible it's a good idea to continue with the same doctor your grandchild had before she came into your care, if the doctor was competent and had a good rapport with her. Keeping the same doctor means that he or she has a file of previous health concerns and appointments on hand, and is already familiar with any challenges the child may have. If you're unable to keep the same doctor then request that the child's previous doctor sends the files to her new doctor. When you visit, bring copies of any medical or family records you have so that he or she can review them at the time of your appointment.

Before you visit with the doctor it's a good idea to note beforehand any questions you have for him or her and to record any behaviours your grandchild exhibits that you're unsure of. Maybe she shouts at you and you don't know why, or maybe she often has trouble doing her homework. Talking to your family doctor about these issues will allow you to jointly map out the best course of action for your grandchild. If your grandchild's birth mother has an alcohol addiction and you suspect she drank while pregnant, then you might talk to your doctor about having the child see a specialist for an assessment of risk for FASD. If your grandchild is having speech and language troubles you may wish to have a referral to a speech pathologist. Bring any questions you have to the appointment and don't feel guilty or awkward for reading your notes in front of a family doctor or specialist. It's better than remembering the question you wanted to ask after the appointment is over.

---

[6]Some of the information in this section is taken from *Adoption Piece by Piece: A Toolkit for Parents* (2003), published by Groundwork Press (www.groundworkpress.com).

WHAT TO DO & BRING TO A DOCTOR'S APPOINTMENT ___

A journal of your child's doctor's appointments, treatments, articles, letters, and therapy sessions

Pass on information you've learned through your own research to your health care professionals; arrive at appointments with as much information as possible that you've found on your own and ask lots of questions; remember that some professional may not be receptive to your ideas, so be persistent and try to respectfully get your point across

Find out past and current health conditions of each birth parent including any mental health diagnoses and genetic disorders in the extended families

Find out the lifestyle details of your grandchild's parents

Record of immunizations

List of all past major medical diagnoses, allergies, medications, injuries and discharge summaries for any hospitalizations

Copies of any specialist consultations

Summaries of any psychiatric hospitalization or treatment

Copies of special education evaluations, school records and individual education plans

Records of dental care or procedures

Assessments of risk for prenatal drug or alcohol exposure

Evidence of any past physical, emotional or sexual abuse; this could include reports written by your social worker, files from a counselling session, or your own written observations

Assessments of risk for HIV, hepatitis B and C, and sexually transmitted diseases

Special Needs

As a grandparent taking care of your grandchild, you might not yet be aware of his medical conditions or challenges related to his past. The child may exhibit behaviours without you knowing the cause. He may be suffering from two or three challenges that have previously gone undiagnosed. Or, the child may have been misdiagnosed or diagnosed for only one challenge when he might have more than one. It could also be that he might have been diagnosed with a disorder or illness, but that the treatment is not working. Depending on the child's age, he might have a history of treatments and medications. In this case it is important for you as the prime caregiver to know as much as you can about the child's family history to determine a cause for any difficulties and to pass these details on to your family doctor and/or specialist.

Many grandparents have grandchildren with special needs ranging from ADD and FAS to spina bifida, cerebral palsy, cystic fibrosis, and adolescent depression (for more information on different conditions, please see Chapter 4 in Part 2 on special needs). It is important that your family doctor not only understands the behaviours and history of your grandchild, but also the physical and psychological effects on you as a result of the child's condition.

An accurate diagnosis will help you and your healthcare professional better plan for the child's needs and care. Early diagnosis is recommended to help maximize the potential outcome for the child. For instance, even mild hearing loss in one ear can affect speech and language development. Obtaining a comprehensive medical and neurodevelopmental assessment of a child who has special needs is the first step for grandparents (for a more detailed description of possible assessment areas and development stages, please see the Assessment Checklist and Development Table in Part 3: Workbook). Understanding deficits early on such as speech or language delays, cognitive and intellectual delays, and psychological and sensory-motor impairments will help determine the most suitable treatment and set the child on the right path. As well, remember that many children who have special needs are at high risk for developing other disorders and diseases.

If your grandchild is seeing a new doctor closer to his new home, it's important to keep him or her up to speed on what special needs challenges your grandchild has, if any. When you visit the doctor explain your grandchild's behaviours and family history. If a syndrome or illness is suspected, the doctor will need to refer you to a specialist. Is there a relevant specialty clinic nearby? If not, do funds exist to cover child and/or caregiver travel costs?

The Internet can be a great resource for current information about various special needs. It offers many online and printed resources that list proven strategies and offer expert help. Information sources include organizations and associations dedicated to particular disorders, such as the Autism Society of British Columbia. These organization websites often have up-to-date information on disorders and behaviours from medical journals, prominent newspapers and magazines. Many of these organizations have library resources that can be accessed by grandparents seeking information on a particular disorder or caregiving strategy. Please remember, however, that any course of action you find on the Internet that you think might work for your grandchild should always be discussed with your doctor first as not all treatments work for every child.

When your grandchild comes to live with you, some of his behaviours might strike you as troubling. It could be that your grandchild has night terrors. Perhaps you suspect him of being abused sexually and you feel a doctor should examine him. Whatever the issue, it's important to talk it over with your doctor and schedule an examination.

ASSESSMENTS TO REQUEST FOR YOUR GRANDCHILD

Complete physical examination

Growth and nutritional conditions

Examination for scars, bruises or other evidence of past abuse

Genital examination of any child suspected of having been sexually abused

Examination for features of FAS or other alcohol-related conditions

Dental evaluation

Immunization update

Age-appropriate screening tests (i.e. vision, hearing)

Screening tests for infectious diseases

Complete developmental and educational evaluation (educational assessments may be available through your school)

Mental health assessment

Mental Health Issues

If there has been abuse, whether it is physical, emotional, sexual or verbal, it's very important to have your family doctor refer you to a professional therapist for your grandchild. When he or she does, ask what training they have, how long they've been a therapist and whether they are registered or licensed. Also, what about costs? Do you have any extended health benefits or know a potential third party who could help you with the therapist's fees? Is there a program you can access through your social worker or your local family centre?

It is important to choose a counselling professional carefully, as opposed to choosing one simply because he or she is covered by the Medical Services Plan or your extended health care. The therapist that you select should be sensitive to your situation, as well as have adequate skills and experience in working with your child's particular needs.

HOW TO CHOOSE A THERAPIST

Think about what issues you would like to work on

Ask the therapist whether he or she has had any experience working with these issues

What continuing clinical training does he or she have on your child's special needs?

Ask the therapist how he or she would work with someone with these difficulties (i.e. working with a child who lives with his grandmother and rarely sees his birthparents)

Does the therapist have experience or interest in working within an integrated case management model (i.e. collaborating with school personnel, youth worker, etc.)?

Is there a charge for the initial consultation session?

Can the fee be reviewed or re-negotiated if your financial situation changes?

How much notice is expected if you need to change an appointment?

Will you be charged for missed appointments?

When and how does the therapist want to be paid for the session(s)?

It's often difficult to navigate the healthcare system for your own health needs not to mention for those of your grandchild. Be well informed about your grandchild's medical history and health, ask lots of questions and remember that doctors don't always know everything. If you're not sure about something then ask questions until you feel you understand. Read up on various health concerns you may have and get a second and third opinion until you're satisfied. After all, you want your grandchild to have the best chance at optimum health for now and for the future.

Your Grandchild's Education
It's been a long time since you had a child in school, and many things have changed. Parents are now more involved in the educational process than ever before, and are expected to contribute to the development of Individual Education Plans (IEPs). If your grandchild has special needs or other challenges, it's important to be aware of what you can ask for, and what you're entitled to in the public school system.

You can request a team meeting with your grandchild's teachers to discuss how your grandchild will learn best, or to discuss any special teaching strategies you think the school would benefit from. It's a good idea to request a full educational assessment for your grandchild, which will test things like his language and motor skills, and should include a psycho-educational assessment. Because of school budget constraints, assessments are not easy to come by, and they will not likely be repeated every year. It's possible that your grandchild will only be assessed one time, and his progress will be monitored from that point on in the classroom only.

Communicate what you think is the best way for your child to learn and what you would like to see achieved in the classroom. Remember that teachers and school administrators often feel attacked by parents who blame them for a multitude of setbacks. Keep your tone reasonable and always be respectful and patient, even while being persistent. Some grandparents find it useful to bring along a relative or trusted friend to these meetings for moral support, but also to act as a secretary. Often, the things the education professionals are saying to you can make you feel like your grandchild's issues are all your fault. Because you are so eager to see your grandchild do well, any setback can trigger a whole host of emotions, from guilt to anger to defensiveness. Your secretary can record exactly what is said; you can read the transcript later on when your emotions have had a chance to clear and you are in a better position to take in information and make decisions.

After this assessment, your child will receive an IEP, which will determine the way your grandchild will be taught for the remainder of the year. You do not have to accept this IEP in its entirety; if you have a problem with one or more of its components, request another team meeting to discuss your concerns. It's important to keep communicating regularly with your grandchild's teachers. You may be surprised to learn that the teachers may have a very persuasive reason for including a certain portion of the IEP. Or, you may be surprised that they agree with you and amend the plan to your suggestions.

Team meetings with professionals and parent/teacher conferences are just as important as your grandchild enters high school and the higher grades. Discuss openly and honestly any problems you may be having scheduling homework times or having your grandchild complete assignments, and be open to listening to the teachers' frustrations as well. It may very well be that you have the perfect solution to a possible behaviour problem that disturbs the classroom.

You may find that in the daily workings of the classroom that your grandchild's teachers will make references to moms and dads, or ask the children to embark on a project featuring the kind of nuclear family that you don't have. If this kind of thing becomes a problem and upsets your grandchild, then have a discussion with the teacher and point out that an effort has to be made to include your grandchild and the family configuration he has.

For more on how to deal with professionals to get the services you need, please see Chapter 6 in Part 2: Advocacy.

ADVOCACY

Phone people. Ask family for help. Talk to your church family. Or, just start looking in the phone book for support groups, medical help, legal professionals. This is the only way that one can obtain help. Do not keep these problems in.

—Carol, caregiver grandparent

Advocating[7] on behalf of you and your grandchild, which means asking for what you need from government, schools and medical professionals until you get it, isn't easy. Perhaps your daughter wasn't always able to care for her child and you were asked with little warning to fulfill a temporary caregiver role. The lines of family authority became blurred and confused. Now that you're the primary caregiver, you might feel guilt and shame because you're focusing on your grandchild instead of your adult child. In addition, you might not have parented children for 20 years or more. The world has changed, and so has the school, legal, and medical systems. In order to advocate effectively—so that your grandchild is healthy, learns at school, and is protected—it is important for you to understand how these different systems work. Navigating the support services in your community—such as counselling, respite care, mentoring, tutoring, activities for grandchildren, informative resources, and assistance for legal, financial and housing issues—requires an ability to advocate. For specific descriptions of these systems go to Part 2: Caregiver 101, Chapter 5: Systems.

What is Advocacy?
Advocacy is closely linked to support. In order to get the supports and services you need

---

[7] Some of the information in this section is taken from *Adoption Piece by Piece: A Toolkit for Parents* (2003), published by Groundwork Press (www.groundworkpress.com).

for yourself and your grandchild, you are often called upon to advocate, which means that you may have to lobby systems and stick up for what's right for her, yourself and the family. Advocacy can also be a form of support. You could choose to be an advocate for another grandparent in need, for example, or ask someone else (i.e. friend or family member) to advocate for you when the battle seems too big to face alone.

You may equate advocacy with being pushy, a rabblerouser or a bully. Or, you may fear that you will attract negative attention from childcare services by speaking out, even if you're speaking up for your grandchild's best interests. It's important to remember that there's a difference between aggressiveness and assertiveness. Effective advocacy has more to do with being assertive than being aggressive. It means doing your research and looking for possible solutions and therapies that could help with your grandchild's issues. It also means considering the professionals' point of view and respecting their opinion even if you don't agree with it. Think about what would be best for your grandchild and make a commitment to do what it takes to see that she gets it. Gather all the fact and statistics you can because while it may be easy to dismiss your opinion as a caregiver, it's far more difficult for a professional to dismiss the findings of a researcher in the same field. Also, remember to keep detailed records of every meeting so that you can refer to these later on if promises have not been kept or if you need to back up your own opinion with someone else's.

Perhaps you feel that your grandchild should have a special education teacher with her in the classroom two days a week. You arrange to meet with the principal and the principal tells you that it won't be possible for the coming year. Instead of raising your voice and telling her that you're outraged and will take the child to another school, you read a list your grandchild's teacher has compiled about the child's difficulty learning. You provide facts and research findings about how early assistance in the classroom stops negative behaviours from occurring later on, and you tell the principal that you've spoken to a special education teacher who works in the school and has an opening two days a week to see your grandchild. This is an example of being assertive as opposed to aggressive. Whatever you do, refrain from calling the professional names or being cruel. Belittling the other person only increases his or her anger and does not help you achieve your goals.

Systems

Not long after your grandchild comes to stay with you, you'll have to deal with systems in order to see that she is taken care of. You will have on-going contact with the health care system, from your grandchild's annual medical check-up to special assessments and support for special needs conditions. When your child hits school age, the education system enters your lives. Even those who home-school children don't escape the system entirely, as they still have to report back to the government and follow provincial curriculum guidelines. It is also possible that you'll have contact with the legal system if a restraining order is needed for an out-of-control parent or if your adolescent grandchild has broken the law or has to appear as a witness in court.

If your grandchild has any special needs it will be more challenging to confront these systems as some professionals are not sensitized to kinship and special needs issues. This can make contact with them challenging, frustrating and overwhelming for both you and your grandchild. Many dealings with systems such as healthcare and education seem way too daunting to take on, and can leave you feeling like a number when you don't get the results you hope for. But as a grandparent who knows your grandchild, you are likely the best person to advocate on behalf of your grandchild. It is possible to survive and effect change within these seemingly immovable systems, even if only one step at a time.

You can start by educating those individuals who have contact with your grand-child—begin with those closest to the situation, such as the teachers and family doctors, and work your way up to higher levels of management—such as school principals or even managers for your local health board—if you're still not getting what you want. The ability to work effectively with these individuals may be difficult, but is critical. Let them know that you're the primary caregiver and that you want what's best for your grandchild. Tell them that you're willing to cooperate with them to ensure your grandchild is safe and excels in all areas of her life to the best of her ability. You don't need to go into detail (unless it is necessary) about why your adult child isn't continuing his or her parenting duties. What's important is that they know you have your grandchild's best interests at heart and that you'd like them to be on board to advocate for her.

Where to Start?

Where do you find the services you're looking for? How do you tap into existing supports? How do you create your own? To be an advocate for your grandchild you need to arm yourself with information that tells you of the child's history. Obtain all your grandchild's records—school, medical, and psychiatric. Look them over and highlight any pertinent information. At her school there may be several files you need to get. The main office has the regular school file. Some schools keep discipline records in a separate file. You'll need to ask. If your grandchild is in special education, the teacher responsible for the IEP keeps a separate file. Also, there should be another file at the district's special education office. Related *services personnel* such as a school psychologist will also have records of instruction for their particular services.

Advocating for you and your grandchild isn't about going it alone. Although you need to know a certain amount to move forward, it's important to reach out to others who can help you as you struggle for the services your grandchild desperately needs. Look for support groups in your area that gather together grandparents helping each other to self-advocate. There are child advocates whose job it is to champion your cause within a system and community advocacy groups that offer help outside the system such as the BC

Self Advocacy Foundation and the BC Aboriginal Network on Disability Society. You can also tap into the support of an informal advocate—such as the friend who walks into the principal's office at your side when you lobby for better supports for your child at school. Access warm lines to connect to services. If there aren't any programs in your area for the kinds of specific needs your grandchild requires then contact your community centre or local support group and suggest they offer an activity or service targeted specifically to grandchildren like yours.

Take Care of Yourself
And in the midst of all your advocacy work, don't forget to take care of yourself to avoid burnout (for more information on self-care, see Part 2, Chapter 7: Care for Caregivers). It's easy to lose sight of your own needs when you're preoccupied with meeting your grandchild's needs on a day-to-day basis. But taking good care of yourself is also a crucial part of your job. After all, you are probably the most important person in your grandchild's world. How can you effectively support your grandchild if you burn out yourself? Here are a few things to consider when advocating on behalf of your grandchild.

SELF-CARE IDEAS

Don't isolate yourself

Get supports in place

Surround yourself by people who understand

Have a list of safe people to call

Do something physical — walk, jog, swim

Get some fresh air

If you have the money, buy yourself something special

Give yourself time to do nothing

Laugh lots

Don't forget to breathe

Let the crisis pass

Let go

CARE FOR THE CAREGIVER

Do not isolate yourself. Take a deep breath and think about how to answer emotionally fraught questions from your grandchildren. Make time for yourself. Smile. Surround yourself with happy people. You love this child or you wouldn't have stepped in. Be proud, yet humble, and know you are doing what is best for that child. You are making a difference.
—Karen, caregiver grandparent

Grandparent caregivers[8], usually focused on the needs of their grandchildren, often have a hard time recognizing and addressing their own needs. Perhaps you're so exhausted that you just don't have the energy to assess your personal health, which, as you grow older, seems to be declining a little bit everyday as you complete the demanding tasks you must perform in order to parent your grandchildren. Perhaps you feel that there just isn't enough time in the day for you to treat yourself to some time alone to take a hot bath or read the latest mystery novel. Many grandparents are experiencing *burden* (when you're managing many overwhelming responsibilities) as well as *burnout* (when you feel that you're unable to go on in your role as a caregiver).

Many grandparents tough it out alone and silently, feeling that they don't have the right to vocalize their concerns or even take care of themselves. All of their emotional, physical and financial resources are spent on their grandchildren, and there is usually nothing left over for relaxation or "me" time. And even when there's enough time or energy in the day

---

[8] Much of the information in this section is taken from *Adoption Piece by Piece: A Toolkit for Parents* (2003), published by Groundwork Press, as well as from the Fall 2004 issue of *Family Groundwork* magazine. Back issues are available at www.groundworkpress.com.

to focus on self-care, grandparents often feel guilty for using it, and instead use that time to perform all those household tasks that never really go away.

Causes of Caregiver Grandparent Burnout and Stress

If you're parenting your grandchild, you have experienced a loss of some kind. Perhaps your daughter has passed away and you're grieving her death. Perhaps your son is living a high risk lifestyle and is involved with drugs and criminal activity; consequently, you're grieving the lost dreams you may have had for your child's adult life. These feelings of grief and loss are only the beginning of the stressors that can chip away at your emotional and physical well-being.

As a caregiver grandparent, you may feel that society in general doesn't understand you, that your role is seen by others as strange. In addition, your friends and some members of your family may not support you in the way you would like, and you could find yourself feeling isolated and lonely. Your friends may not want to socialize with you and your young grandchildren. Your other adult children may be angry at their sibling's inability to parent his or her children and they may feel that you've made a bad decision in taking the children on. The isolation you experience doesn't help your feelings of stress, and you might feel that you and the grandchildren are all alone, and must muddle through your problems by yourselves.

Trying to make the best of things, you make some calls and ask different agencies if there are any supports or resources you could use to ease your burden. The more you look, however, the more depressed you feel; you soon realize that there are very few government-supported programs for grandparents like you. Your feelings of loneliness grow more intense.

Many grandparents are at the tail end of their working years, and many are retired already. Their incomes are often just enough to support their lifestyles and not much more. When grandchildren come into the picture and parenting necessities like diapers, school supplies and braces need to be purchased, many grandparents have great difficulty finding the funds to cover the extra expenses. Perhaps you have to move because your apartment is too small or doesn't allow children. If your grandchild has special needs, you may have to find some money to pay for therapy programs or specialized equipment. Maybe you even have to return to work in order to help with the mounting pile of bills. Compensation from government programs like the Temporary Care program administered by Ontario Works only scratch the surface.

Grandparents often live with the fear that their grandchildren will be taken away from them at any moment by child welfare authorities or by their biological parents. Because grandparents are older, they also fear that they will one day be unable to care for their grandchildren because of illness or death. These fears, which can constantly be in the back of your mind, increase stress levels an enormous amount.

You may feel anger toward your adult child for leaving you with the responsibility of caring for his or her child. Or, you may feel you are to blame for your child's lack of parenting skills. Perhaps your grandchild has special needs that require more of your attention than you had bargained for. You are overworked and your body, not as young as it once was, is responding badly to the increased level of work. It would be great if you could send the children to daycare once in a while, but you might be afraid that their special needs would be ignored by a childcare provider. Also, considering all the things you've had to buy lately for your grandchildren, you're not sure you could afford it.

Children who have experienced upheaval and who have not had happy pasts as the result of abuse or neglect, often feel angry or confused. You may be spending a lot of your time trying to deal with your grandchild's fears or acting-out, and this kind of intensive work leaves you feeling exhausted and fed up. And, perhaps you're not sure how to deal with your grandchild's needs; after all, a lot has changed since you parented your adult children. HIV/AIDS, the availability of drugs, the violence and sex that are on TV everyday—all these are things that cause you to worry over the safety and well-being of your grandchildren. As well, parenting itself has changed. You're no longer sure if spanking is acceptable and consequently you feel paralyzed when it comes to discipline. It's no wonder that grandparents caring for their grandchildren often feel that they are at the end of their rope.

Recognizing the Signs of Burnout

Anxiety and responsibility play a huge part in caregiver burnout, and can manifest as physical conditions. Grandparents often overlook their diets and experience changes in appetite and weight due to eating too much or too little, or eating unhealthily. Stress can lead to headaches, stomach and digestion problems, fatigue, insomnia, back and neck pain, loss of energy and increased drug and alcohol use. Common health problems among grandparents who are caring for their grandchildren include diabetes, high blood pressure, high cholesterol and fluctuating weight. Existing conditions, like angina or asthma, can flare up and become worse than ever.

Caregiver grandparents often overlook their emotional needs as well. They can experience irritability, concentration and memory problems, social isolation, and, more seriously, depression. You may feel the urge to run away from your problems by hiding or sleeping more than usual. Often, stressed grandparents may cry frequently and experience an inability to find humour in everyday situations. You may even feel a loss of purpose, and begin questioning why you're taking care of your grandchildren at all. Or, you may be striving to reach some kind of unrealistic perfection with your home and family and feeling frustration because it's unattainable.

Activities to Help Combat Burnout and Stress

Clearly, your health as a caregiver affects the health of your entire family. In order to have a strong relationship with your spouse, and enough energy to care for your grandchildren, you have to make time for yourself and for the things you enjoy. Although caregiving is a big part of who you are, it's not your only role in life and it's important that you take the time to step out of that caregiver role regularly.

First, take care of your health. If you're tempted to cancel a doctor's appointment because of time constraints or a situation at home, don't. Caregiver grandparents often ignore their physical health; this is especially dangerous if your health was not great to begin with and if, as you get older, you're experiencing more and more discomfort or pain. Learn to self-monitor and recognize signs of fatigue, frustration and depression. By eating right and paying close attention to your health, you're setting an excellent example to your grandchildren, who will also learn to take good care of themselves.

Following are some guidelines ("Checkups and Prevention" 2006), on what health tests to ask for and how often, particularly if you're over 50. Keep in mind that this is a

ROUTINE HEALTH TESTS TO KEEP IN MIND

rough guide only and that you should always check with your family doctor on how often you need to undergo routine tests.

Colonoscopy: once a year

Blood pressure: once every three years, more if you have blood pressure problems

Blood glucose: once every three years

Cholesterol: every five years, more if you have had problems with cholesterol in the past

Flu vaccination: once a year

Mammogram: once a year

PAP smear: once a year

Prostate exam: once a year

Cut back on foods high in fat, sugar and salt, and concentrate on eating lots of fruit and vegetables, lean protein like skinless chicken and high-fibre grains like brown rice and granola. Try to stay away from fast and processed food and instead stock your kitchen with healthy and easy snacks like raisins, carrot sticks, yogurt and almonds. Incorporate some kind of fun exercise into your routine, even if that means just walking briskly around your local park for 20 minutes.

Seek support from your community, either from respite care providers, support services or more informally through your family and friends. Surround yourself with people who understand your situation and whom you can count on to listen to your feelings. Take 15 to 20 minutes everyday to focus on yourself and do something you enjoy (take a bath, read the funnies, take a nap) and schedule a couple of hours a week away from your grandchildren and your household responsibilities. Make sure you get enough sleep. Buy yourself some time by deciding which tasks need to be done right now and which ones can be finished later. Treat yourself, whether that means making yourself your favourite omelette or going out to see a movie. Learn to say no when others ask you to commit to other projects—remember, it's okay to refuse to do something just because you don't want to.

STRATEGIES

A Quick Breathing Exercise to Help You Relax

As babies we breathe naturally, but as we grow we learn to constrict our bodies as we confront the day-to-day problems that arise. Before you know it, we're holding our breath and not breathing, as we should to be healthy. It may seem like a small thing, but stopping to let air into your lungs can actually mean the difference between "losing it" and "keeping your cool." When the doorbell rings, when your grandchild is shouting at you, when the whole house is an upset of dogs, kids and dirty clothes, here's a quick and easy de-stressor you can practice before you accidentally wash the family cat with the next load of laundry.

This is an exercise you can do anywhere, in any position: sitting, standing or lying down. Exhale deeply, pushing the abdomen in. Inhale slowly and watch, as your belly gets bigger. Keep inhaling and expand the chest. Exhale slowly, making sure that all the air leaves your abdomen and chest. Are you feeling more relaxed already? Three cheers for stopping long enough to breathe!

Talk Therapy: a Communication Exercise

Talk therapy is a fancy term for talking about what is bothering you. This effective form of therapy can be practiced with a trusted friend, spouse, talking circle or therapist. Talking about what's bothering you can help you pinpoint the things that are causing difficulty in your life. Sometimes it helps to discuss personal challenges with another person who might have an entirely different perspective. But even if they don't, the simple act of voicing your feelings will help you to feel less stressed and more in control.

The Stress Journal Exercise

Keep a journal of things that bother you during the day. Or, make a list of all the things that stress you out. How do they affect you? Do they keep you awake, or make you worry? Every time you write an entry, select one of the things on your list and decide to do something about it. Maybe you can't change the time you get up in the morning, but you might be able to change other things that make it so difficult for you to get the day started, such as moving up the time the children go to bed. You can also control how you react to each situation. Slowly chipping away at the list and making small changes will help you feel more in control and able to face issues as they arise.

Respite

Respite care is the childcare you arrange for your grandchildren so that you can have some time to yourself. There are several ways of setting up respite care for your family—some formal and some informal. Some Canadian provinces offer respite care services to families who are involved with the child welfare system. If you have a kinship care agreement with your local agency, or are caring for your grandchild as a foster parent, you may have access to these services. Also, you may be eligible for free childcare if you can prove a financial need. Check your local child welfare office, or inquire at a community or family centre, many of which operate these kinds of programs.

Informal respite can mean scheduling a day away from your grandchildren. Arrange for a trusted friend or relative to provide childcare—this is especially important if your grandchild has behavioural issues, or disabilities that need special attention. If you know other parents or grandparents, you could provide a day of childcare yourself in exchange. Also make plans for longer-term care during weekends or holidays once a year or for however often you think you'll need.

If you do end up hiring a babysitter or other professional, prepare him or her thoroughly for any issue that may come up. If your grandchild is affected by FASD, for example, go over the child's schedule with the babysitter, impressing on him or her, the importance of a predictable, structured timetable.

Prepare your grandchild for the respite as well by taking him or her to meet the respite provider before the scheduled visit and outlining exactly what his or her day will be like. If your grandchild has trouble with change, or experiences anxiety when not with you, you may have to schedule several visits with the potential care provider that you and your grandchild participate in together. As the child grows more comfortable with this other adult, you can leave him or her for short, and then longer periods of time until your grandchild can be left alone comfortably. Although this takes a certain amount of effort, in the end, this break will help you be the best caregiver you can be. It will also help your grandchild with any social or abandonment issues he or she may have.

Remember to have fun during your time away from your grandchildren—don't fall into cleaning the house or catching up on laundry. This time is for you to decompress, so take advantage of it!

3

We are not funded or supported by the government. So for any strategies or supports, I have to find them myself, whether it is financial or trying to get an appointment with the right specialist or putting the girls into the right programs after school or just dealing with the school system. These are my challenges on an everyday level.
—Carol, caregiver grandparent

DEVELOPMENT TABLES

It's a good idea to keep track of how your grandchild is developing[9], particularly if you think she might have special needs or challenges associated with the time she spent with her parents or previous caregivers. Below are tables outlining typical physical, motor, language, social and cognitive development. Keep in mind that the information in these table is not to be used in place of the advice of a doctor. If you have any questions about your grandchild's development, please contact a health care professional.

Physical Development						
	Birth to 4 months	4 to 8 months	8 to 12 months	12 to 18 months	18 to 24 months	2 to 5 years
	Sleeps 15 to 20 hours daily	Develops schedule for sleeping, eating, being awake	Sleeps 11 to 13 hours a night, with 1 or 2 naps during day	May show interest in toilet training	Gains some control of bowels and bladder	Toilet trained, goes without reminder
Weight	10 to 18 lbs.	14 to 23 lbs.	17 to 27 lbs.	17 to 30 lbs.	20 to 32 lbs.	28 to 55 lbs.
Height	23 to 27 inches	25 to 30 inches	27 to 32 inches	27 to 35 inches	30 to 37 inches	22 to 45 inches

[9]This section is taken from *Living with Prenatal Drug Exposure: A Guide for Parents* (2003) published by Groundwork Press. Copies are available at www.groundworkpress.com.

Gross Motor Skills*					
Birth to 4 months	4 to 8 months	8 to 12 months	12 to 18 months	18 to 24 months	2 to 5 years
Lifts head and chest when lying on stomach	Rolls from stomach to back and back to stomach	Crawls	Stands without support	Climbs stairs	Rides tricycle
Kicks with legs	Sits alone without support	Pulls self to standing position, may walk with support	Walks unaided for longer intervals (up to 20 minutes)	Runs, kicks ball	Skips, stands on one leg, jumps over greater distances, walks down stairs without difficulty

*Gross motor skills refers to the ability to control large, general movements like walking, waving or jumping.

Fine Motor Skills**					
Birth to 4 months	4 to 8 months	8 to 12 months	12 to 18 months	18 to 24 months	2 to 5 years
Grasps rattle or finger	Sucks hands or individual fingers	Holds objects between finger and thumb	Holds pencil and scribbles, turns pages in books	Feeds self with spoon	Draw person
Clasps hands together	Grasps objects with both hands	Begins to feed self with finger foods	Builds short tower of blocks	Opens drawers, cabinets, doors	Dress self with little or no help

**Fine motor skills refers to the ability to control small, precise movements like pointing or grasping.

Speech & Language					
Birth to 4 months	4 to 8 months	8 to 12 months	12 to 18 months	18 to 24 months	2 to 5 years
Turns head and responds to voices	Imitates speech, jabbers	Waves good-bye	Understands sentences and commands	Speech can be understood half of the time	Speech completely understandable
Squeals, laughs, coos	Responds to name	Uses "Dada" and "Mama"	Formulates 2-word sentences	Knows names of familiar objects	Able to define words and name opposites

Social-Emotional Development					
Birth to 4 months	4 to 8 months	8 to 12 months	12 to 18 months	18 to 24 months	2 to 5 years
Cries to communicate displeasure	Differentiates between scolding and playing	Imitates others' activities	Helps with housework	Develops sense of self, uses "mine"	Able to separate from caregiver without crying
Responds with smiles	Responds to familiar people, shows fear with strangers	Offers toys to others, expects them back	Upset when separated from caregiver	Throws temper tantrums	Identifies own feelings, names friends

Cognition***					
Birth to 4 months	4 to 8 months	8 to 12 months	12 to 18 months	18 to 24 months	2 to 5 years
Explores with mouth	Focuses on and reaches for objects	Finds object after watching it being hidden	Plays simple make believe	Assigns functions to toys (toy car carries doll to work)	Differentiates between truth and fiction
Plays with hands and feet	Uses same behaviour for all objects (puts in mouth, bang, etc.)	Plays peek-a-boo	Searches for hidden objects	Understand that one action causes another (pressing TV button turns it on)	Creates make believe situations, assigns roles to self and others

***Cognition refers to intellectual and causal development.

ASSESSMENT CHECKLIST

The following is a list[10] of developmental areas you can have assessed for your grandchild if you're concerned that he might have challenges. Please note that this list is to be used as a guide only and that assessments should be performed by a qualified medical professional. If you have any questions regarding your grandchild's development, please contact your doctor.

Physical Health	Development	Behaviour	Environment
General health	Language	Temperament	It's important to assess your grandchild's environment (home, school, play, friends, family) to see if these might be affecting development as well.
Physical maturation	Learning	Adaptive skills	
Growth	School performance	Coping skills	
Nutrition	Motor skills	Interpersonal relations	
Motor skills	Attention	Self-esteem	
Reflexes	Organization	Task performance	
Coordination	Social skills	Emotional, cognitive status	

See *Developmental-Behavioral Pediatrics*, by Melvin Levine, et al, (bibliographic information included at the back of this guide) for a more detailed assessment table.

---

[10]This section is taken from *Living with Prenatal Drug Exposure: A Guide for Parents* (2003) published by Groundwork Press. Copies are available at www.groundworkpress.com.

SELF-CARE CHECKLIST

Grandparents who parent a second time often experience health problems related to stress. Some complain of headaches, chronic aches and pains, or stomach troubles. Many talk about constantly being tired, and having difficulty doing all that is required of them. This might include waking up early to take a granddaughter to school, working two jobs to make ends meet, and having to drive your grandson to hockey practice a couple of mornings a week.

Although you might be in good health, re-parenting is not the same as parenting the first time. You probably get tired more easily. Maybe loud noises bother you more, or you feel you need more time to yourself. Taking care of your needs means not waiting for little health troubles to snowball into big ones. If you become unwell, it will be very difficult to attend to your grandchild's needs in the future.

The following is a list that focuses on self-care. Consult it often. Copy it down and stick it on the fridge, or in a personal area above your desk or beside your bed. Don't worry how many items you complete on the list. Try for one or two, and then gradually increase the number of self-care tasks you perform each day. And, give yourself a big pat on the back for trying!

TAKING CARE OF YOURSELF

Eat right. Cut down on fatty meats, fast and processed foods, and eat lots of fruits and vegetables to make sure you get your vitamins and minerals.

Go to your yearly checkups. Visit your family doctor once a year for a physical and more if you have a health concern.

Seek respite. Join a support group and share child care with other grandparents, or contact your local childcare office for information on respite care in your area.

Treat yourself. Go to a movie once a month, schedule a back massage or pedicure—you deserve it!

Keep your cool. Anger intensifies stress and can increase your blood pressure. Express your feelings calmly and clearly, and try not to fly off the handle.

Remember to breathe. When we focus on our breathing, it's amazing how we react more positively to outside stresses.

Take time for yourself. Find a quiet spot in your home to be by yourself. Try 15 minutes at first and increase the amount of time gradually.

Laugh lots. A good belly laugh can lower blood pressure, boost the immune system, reduce stress and protect the heart. Take time each day to see humour in situations that arise. And laughing with others is doubly good for you!

Get support. Join a support group or Aboriginal talking circle, talk to sympathetic friends often, or see a counsellor if needed. Be social when you can and connect to community supports.

KEEPING TRACK

When caring for your grandchild, it's important to keep track[11] of everything. When you're advocating for services, arranging for custody or discussing with professionals which strategies are most effective for your grandchild, having a record of when, where, what and why for every meeting, appointment and behaviour is very valuable. Detailed notes make a good impression and will help professionals take you seriously.

The Professional Meeting Log, Behavioural Log and Visitation Log in this section are designed to help you keep track of all events and behaviours that relate to your grandchild. Be aware that these are only guides; feel free to change them to suit your needs.

---

[11]This section is taken, in part, from *Living with Prenatal Drug Exposure: A Guide for Parents* (2003) published by Groundwork Press. Copies are available at www.groundworkpress.com.

Professional Meeting Log

Use this log to keep track of all the meetings you have with professionals (doctors, lawyers, social workers, teachers, etc.). Remember to also keep copies of all pertinent documents such as assessment results and report cards.

Professional

_____

Date & time

_____

Topics discussed

_____

_____

_____

Resolutions/Plan of action agreed upon

_____

_____

_____

_____

_____

Next meeting scheduled for

_____

Additional documents filed under

_____

_____

Notes

_____

_____

_____

_____

_____

Behavioural Log

Use this log to keep track of behaviours to get a clear idea of what works and doesn't work for your grandchild.

Date & time

_____

Observed behaviour

_____

Situation preceding behaviour

_____

_____

Signs of distress preceding behaviour

_____

_____

Behaviour resolved by

_____

_____

Behaviour exacerbated by

_____

_____

Notes

_____

_____

_____

_____

_____

Visitation Log

Use this log to record details of your grandchild's visits with his parents. These kinds of records can be very useful for any custody issues that may come up, or if you think it necessary at some point to obtain a restraining order against your adult child (please see Part 2: Caregiver 101, Chapter 5: Systems for more information on legal matters).

Name of parent

_____

Date & time of visit

_____

State of mind of parent

_____

 • At pick-up

_____

_____

 • At drop-off

_____

_____

State of mind of grandchild

_____

 • At pick-up

_____

_____

 • At drop-off

_____

_____

Topics discussed

_____

_____

_____

_____

_____

_____

Next visit scheduled for
_____

Notes/concerns
_____

_____

_____

_____

_____

_____

_____

GRANDPARENT TO GRANDCHILD DISCUSSION TOPICS

You may find that because it has been a long time since you raised a child, you are unsure about how to approach difficult subjects with your grandchild. Perhaps your social worker has advised you to talk to your grandchild about her past. Or, perhaps you perceive that your grandchild is experiencing feelings she doesn't understand and that she needs some guidance from you to sort out all the confusion. Your grandchild might approach you herself and ask you questions. Regardless, your grandchild has been through some tough times and needs to talk through her thoughts and emotions, so here are some topics you can discuss with her and some tips on how you can guide the conversation.

Your Grandchild's Birth Parents

If your grandchild's birth parents are still living in high risk situations (i.e. drug or alcohol addiction, criminal involvement, abusive relationships), then your grandchild is likely experiencing feelings of anxiety and abandonment. She may worry about her birth father's health and whereabouts, or she may be wondering what she did that made her parents want to leave her with a grandparent. She may feel intense joy when her parents come to visit, only to feel disappointment and sadness when they don't follow through with promises or stick to a visitation schedule.

What to Say

Be truthful about the parents' lives and issues. This doesn't mean using negative language to explain your child's situation. You don't have to tell your grandchild all the details, but do try to tell her as much as you can in a way that she will understand. For example, when explaining that her birth father is in prison for drug-related reasons, you could say, "Your dad is in jail because he did something wrong and needs to be disciplined, in the same way that you have to have a time-out when you take a toy from your cousin." Being honest keeps your grandchild from harbouring unrealistic fantasies about living again with her parents, or speculating on her own about why her parents are absent from her life.

Reassure your grandchild that her parents' behaviour is not her fault. Often, children who are no longer living with their parents blame themselves for their parents' inability to parent. Your grandchild might think that something she did or said drove her parents away and that they no longer love her. Explain to your grandchild that her parents are going through a hard time right now and that they have to focus on fixing their problems, which is why they can't take care of her. A child needs to feel good about her parents. Any criticism of them will negatively affect a child's self-esteem. Be clear that their problems have nothing to do with her. You can say something like, "Your mother uses drugs and they make her sick. She is trying to stop using them so she can get healthy. You didn't make her sick, the drugs did." Also, explain that her parents still love her and always will, and that nothing your grandchild could ever do would stop them, or you, from loving her.

Explain to your grandchild that her living arrangement isn't your fault either. Some children will feel anger and blame their grandparents for driving their parents away. Your grandchild may feel that she was getting along just fine with her father and that they didn't need you to interfere. Accept her feelings of anger and listen to everything she has to say. After she has calmed down and talked herself out of it, give her the reasons she can't live with her father. Make sure these reasons are tangible and easily understood, and keep your hurt or angry feelings to yourself (you can let them out later when talking to a trusted friend). Perhaps you say something like, "You can't live with your dad because his home wasn't safe. He left you alone with people you barely knew. And he couldn't afford the things you need, like glasses and school supplies." Point out all the positive aspects of living with you, like being able to go to the beach every weekend, or having her own bed to sleep in. While her anger may not totally disappear, she will at least come to see that it's practical for her to live with you. Whatever you do, don't blame the parents when talking with your grandchild by saying things like, "You live with me because your father is a screw-up." This will only further alienate your grandchild.

Acknowledge your grandchild's worries and anxiety. It's perfectly natural for your grandchild to be concerned about her birth parents' welfare. You can acknowledge her feelings by saying, "Of course you worry about your dad; I do too. It's part of loving someone." However, be aware that this anxiety can become a problem when she exhibits some troubling behaviours, like lack of sleep or expressing a desire to run away and find her parents. At this point, it's good to reassure your grandchild that, although her parents have problems, they need the time and space to work through it all themselves. You could say, "Your dad will get help when he needs it. He's a grown-up and the best help you can give him is to love him and tell him that whenever you talk to him."

Past Abuse and Neglect

This is a hard topic. As the grandparent, you feel anger at your grandchild's parents for inflicting abuse, or for exposing your grandchild to an abusive situation. However your grandchild will be experiencing a number of unpleasant and confusing feelings, and it is up to you to help her sort them out in a calm and clear way. For more discussion topics on abuse and neglect, please see Chapter 2: Your Grandchild's Emotions in Part 2: Caregiver 101.

What to Say

Remain calm. You will feel anger, resentment and even disgust whenever you think about the abuse of your grandchild, but when you discuss it with her, it's important to put your own feelings away and focus instead on how your grandchild is feeling. She may express things that upset or disturb you. You might wish to say something like: "I'm sad that happened to you" as this validates that there is an emotional component, yet doesn't focus on your feelings at the expense of hers. Afterward, you can discuss your feelings with another adult, perhaps your spouse, a close friend, a pastor or priest, or a therapist.

Reassure your grandchild that she is safe. Your grandchild may be afraid to express how she feels, especially if she has been punished or abused for expressing feelings before. Or, she may be afraid that her abuser will come back for her. Tell her that your home is a safe place where no one hits anyone else and where everyone respects everybody else's feelings, bodies and personal space. Back this up by remaining reasonable when you have to discipline your grandchild and making sure your consequences for her acting-out are immediate and appropriate to the situation (please see Chapter 3: Parenting Skills in Part 2: Caregiver 101 for discipline ideas). Acknowledge and accept everything she is telling you, from details of the abuse, to her conflicting feelings of love and fear for her abuser. You can say, "All feelings are okay and I'll listen any time you want to tell me about them." Explain that whenever she's feeling bad, she can talk to you instead of acting out through tantrums or through hurting the feelings of others. If she's not able to talk about something try giving her a pillow she can punch to let her anger out.

Help your grandchild sort out conflicting feelings about her abuser. Often, a child's abuser will be a trusted adult, such as a parent, step-parent or friend of the family. Consequently, your grandchild may have conflicting emotions about this abuser, feeling love, fear and hate all at once. Reassure her that her feelings are not wrong, and that the confusion is normal. Attribute her feelings of fear and hate to the abuse as opposed to the abuser, saying, "What he did to you is scary and bad and you can hate the way he made you feel pain. But you can still love him even though he did bad things to you." By separating the abuse from the person, your grandchild will be able to eventually make sense of the conflict.

Help your grandchild through the stages of grief and loss. Your grandchild has lost daily contact with her parents and this is hard and troubling. In order to help her progress through her grieving (for more on grief and loss, see Chapter 2: Your Grandchild's Emotions in Part 2: Caregiver 101), listen to her when she talks of her parents and contribute your own positive memories to the conversation. Accept all the feelings she will express to you, whether they turn out to be sadness, guilt, anger, blame or a combination. Unfortunately, there is no way for you to end your grandchild's grief. However, by allowing her to speak about it, she will be able to let go of these feelings of loss, and eventually move on.

Your Grandchild's Peers

When your grandchild goes to school or socializes with other children, she will soon come to realize that her living situation is not typical, and that most children live with one or two parents, not their grandparents. The other children may tease her or ask her questions that make her uncomfortable. She may feel *different* because some activities that parents do with their children are things that you might not be able to do because of your health, things like coaching a soccer team, or going on class camping trips as a parent chaperone.

What to Say
Explain that every family is different. Point out to your grandchild that every child's family is different. Perhaps she has a friend who lives with only her father or another who is adopted. Or, maybe she knows someone who spends half the week at her mother's house and the other half at her father's house. Explain to her in your own words that living with a grandparent makes her no less and no more different than any other child.

Give your grandchild a stock answer to questions about her family. Your grandchild may choose to be honest and tell her friends all about her parents and grandparents. However, if she is having trouble deciding how to explain her living arrangement to other children, provide her with an explanation that she can use over and over again. Something like, "I live with my grandma because my dad is sick right now." Or, "My mom doesn't have enough money to take care of me everyday, so I moved in with my grandpa." Encourage her to be truthful, but to only reveal the details she is comfortable with.

Teach your grandchild that it's okay not to answer invasive questions. Sometimes, other children and even their parents will pepper your grandchild with questions about her living arrangement. They might ask things like, "Is your father a drug dealer?" Or, "I hear your mother has AIDS. Is that true?" These kinds of questions are not respectful or appropriate, and you can teach your grandchild that she only has to answer them if she wants to. She can respond by saying, "I don't feel comfortable talking about my parents right now." Teach her that responding aggressively is not the answer and will only make the other child angry and more likely to believe hurtful things about her. For instance, something like, "That's none of your business" or "Shut up" will not be helpful.

Difficult Behaviours

There will be times when your grandchild will act out. She may break things or call you names. Or, she might even physically hurt another child or your spouse. After you've disciplined her (for discipline methods, see Chapter 3: Parenting Skills in Part 2: Caregiver 101) and both of you have had some time to cool off, take the time to have a discussion with her about what it is that caused this behaviour.

What to Say
Ask your grandchild if something happened earlier that upset her. Often, an event that left your grandchild feeling angry or sad will be the source of her acting-out. Perhaps her birth mother came by her school and promised that she would find a job and take her to live with her. Maybe one of her friends teased your grandchild about being born a "crack baby." Talk to her about how this made her feel and acknowledge her emotions by saying, "I understand that this makes you angry. It makes me angry too." Do not deny her feelings or tell her that they are inappropriate. For example, it will damage her self-esteem to say something like, "That's nothing to get upset about." Clearly, something has made her upset, so denying the feeling will only prevent your grandchild from expressing any further feelings to you, and to others she becomes close to down the road.

Explain that hurting others or damaging property doesn't make anything better. Encourage your grandchild to come to you when she's upset and talk it through instead of pinching one of her friends or smashing your favourite mug. Back this up by praising her whenever she does express her feelings by saying, "I'm so glad you told me how upset your teacher made you this morning. It makes me feel that you trust and love me." If your grandchild is not ready to express her feelings in words, give her a pillow to punch or some other physical outlet for her emotions that will not hurt her or others.

What if Your Grandchild Doesn't Want to Talk?

Sometimes, children keep their feelings to themselves and simply act out instead. Or, the child who doesn't like to talk about emotions or the past will act like everything is fine and appear to be a model student and grandchild. Clearly, your grandchild has felt pain and has feelings that need to be expressed.

Instead of approaching her and saying, "Let's have a talk" out of the blue, you can try initiating conversation when the moment suggests it. For example, if you're watching the *Harry Potter* movie on TV, you can ask her how she thinks Harry must have felt when his parents died. This conversation could lead into her own feelings about her absent parents. Or, if your grandchild comes home from school and tells you that one of the boys in her class punched another little boy in the face, you could ask her why she thinks he wanted to do that. This could lead to a conversation about her lingering anger toward someone who physically abused her in the past.

If your grandchild is uncomfortable listening to your feelings, you could start a little game where you write notes expressing your feelings about your grandchild and leave them where she will find them such as on her pillow or in her school bag. You could write things like, "I'm proud of you for being so understanding with your friends." Or, "I'm glad you live with me because you help me feel young." Gently encourage her to leave you notes as well.

You can also encourage her to express her feelings in alternative ways, like through drawing or painting, writing poetry, or even through sports or dance. Acknowledge her actions that may be an outlet for feelings by saying things like, "This little girl in your painting seems sad to me. Why is she feeling sad?" Or, "You swam really hard today. Was there something that made you work extra hard?"

WHY I PARENT
MY GRANDCHILD

I firmly believe that grandparents raising grandchildren are giving the children an awesome gift of love and support that can only be given by family. The rewards are daily as our grandchildren tell us they love us and we get to see all their "firsts".
—Betty, caregiver grandparent

In spite of the enormous challenges that grandparents face on a daily basis, most have positive things to say about the experience of parenting a second time. The following is a list of positives that grandparents can read when things get difficult to remind themselves of why they parent (Cornelius 2006).

WHY I GRANDPARENT

Great **satisfaction** in providing care and security

Enjoyment from offering grandchildren what they need and the best care possible

Respect from the community

Ability to give **unconditional love**

Possibility of having a **spiritual influence** on the children

WHY I GRANDPARENT

Giving a sense of **stability and belonging**

Gaining more **appreciation of time** and how precious it is

Becoming stronger advocates for children

Feeling young and active

If we did not take responsibility for them **we would lose access**

Closer connection with the children and with the world

Receiving so much **love from the grandchildren**

Helping **give grandchildren hope** and the encouragement to keep going

Opportunity to **learn new things** all the time

Enhanced sense of **self-empowerment** that comes with parenting

Chance to **be a parent again**

Opportunity to **teach trust**

Learning patience and tolerance

Learning to prioritize demands

Instilling in grandchildren **pride** in who they are

No trouble sleeping!

Sense of **focus** and purpose

Satisfaction in knowing that children are included in cultural events and exposed to their **cultural heritage**

Opportunity to **experience child's "firsts"** and successes

Opportunity to **witness child's transformation from scared to joyful**

SUPPORT GROUP START-UP

By attending support groups, I have come to understand that I am not the only grandparent who faces hardships every day. We can only try to overcome challenges one day at a time; sometimes one moment at a time.

—Carol, caregiver grandparent

Starting a support group[12] might sound like a scary thing to you, especially if you've never done it before. What do you hope to accomplish by starting one? You might be looking for a talking circle to share stories with other grandparents in order to be supported and helped through difficult times. Or you might be interested in incorporating guest speakers who specialize in issues related to legal guardianship or financial assistance. It could be that you simply want to connect with a couple of grandparents to have coffee occasionally, and to sometimes trade off on childcare and other duties.

What's Your Purpose?
When you finally get together with the group of interested grandparents one of the first things to do is develop a statement of purpose. Answer the question: Why are you there and what do you hope to accomplish? It is important to recognize that this purpose will evolve over time as your group evolves. Be prepared to re-visit your purpose statement periodically and keep it current.

Groups have a life cycle (a few months to a few years) and often have a purpose cycle as well. For example, your group may first come together to vent frustration and anger and provide mutual support. Then you may find you want to lobby in your community

---

[12]Some of the information in this section is taken from *Adoption Piece by Piece: A Toolkit for Parents* (2003), published by Groundwork Press (www.groundworkpress.com).

for subsidized childcare for grandparents, or support to deal with school issues related to troubled youth. Having a statement of purpose provides focus for your group and allows you to acknowledge changes in your group's activities. In this case an updated statement of purpose allows you to communicate clearly to new members or others what it is your group does or is about. All groups are unique and each has its own character and form. However, having said that, there are general guidelines that may increase the efficacy of your group.

Who's in Charge?

Most commonly the initial stated purpose for groups coming together is to provide mutual support. But then we need to ask, what is support and how can it be delivered? How is your group going to make decisions related to spending money, where to meet, and what to say in a letter to politicians? There is no perfect and absolute model of governance that fits all situations. The important thing is to find a model that is flexible and works for you and your group. Depending on your purpose, you might select a consensus model of group decision making, which is sometimes referred to as a *kitchen table* model. Another model that might work better is to take on an executive structure whereby there is one leader and a board of directors. Whatever it is, everyone involved should be very clear and comfortable about what the system refers to. And you should have a well-defined method of informing and orienting new group members. This might take the form of a one-pager that you hand out to explain the decision-making style and process of the group.

Whatever your decision-making system, it will probably evolve or change over time. But if you are clear about what the system is then it is also more likely that you will be able to assess whether it is continuing to meet the changing needs of your group. Consequently, you will be able to make changes to your decision making process in a deliberate and appropriate manner as needed. When the structure is clear and well understood by everyone involved, discussion about changes is more likely to be kept to those structures rather than becoming about personalities of those in the group. For instance, in this case you're more likely to hear something such as, "This structure is not working anymore and I suggest these changes," rather than "You are a petty tyrant and I'm not listening to you anymore."

Big or Small

Whether your group is localized in a small community or spread out over many cities has a great impact on decisions that will be made. If your intention is to serve a local area (your town, neighbourhood, community, etc) it makes sense to centralize your services so that members meet at the same place or at least in the same area and that the resources the group accesses are localized. If you are spread out over one whole province, for instance, then dropping in to a central office for a meeting isn't so easy. Also, a kitchen table model of decision making becomes less feasible with members dispersed over such a wide area.

However, recent technological developments such as private discussion forums on the Internet, instant messaging and even simple e-mail, make meeting at a distance easier.

It is useful to have a format or loose structure for your group so you can have a time when you meet for sharing or venting, brainstorming, problem solving, and a time for closure or a menu of formats that the group can chose from to suit its needs at the time. For instance, one meeting might have a problem solving focus while the next may have an informational focus with a guest speaker. It is also useful as a facilitator to stimulate discussion and develop trust and rapport (i.e. by using ice breakers, values clarification, issues exploration, communication, etc.) It is crucial that there be clear guidelines regarding your group's process, acceptable behaviour and general standards including confidentiality issues. For instance, if you live in a small town and one support group member is venting because her daughter is battling alcohol addiction and forgot to pick up her son it's important to know that others won't talk about this outside the group. Or, it is crucial that the speaker in a talking circle can speak uninterrupted and that this rule is communicated to the whole group before a meeting begins.

This standards list should be reviewed from time to time to be sure everyone is clear about what they are and to be sure they are still serving the group's needs. Full understanding and endorsement by the group also means individuals are more likely to be supported if they need to call a member's attention to the standards. For example, if you have an agreed standard for letting everyone have their time to speak and one member is hogging all the group time, it is easier and more likely the group will support you when you ask that member to allow others to speak if it is written in the support group's standards list.

It is particularly important that your group have a process for welcoming new members and of acquainting them with the group standards. If your group feels like a clique that might be hard to crack, a new member is unlikely to stay very long. Your group should as much as possible be kept to a schedule. Rather than let it run on, even if it is exciting, a facilitator needs to stay on top of group process and time lines and begin moving to closure. He or she might say something like, "That's a tough problem. Let's think about it and discuss it further at the next meeting" because group members have expectations and obligations such as childcare. Finally, having your group in a neutral setting such as a community centre or neighbourhood house can preclude negative reactions that may come from the use of private homes. There might be interruptions in private homes and difficulty keeping the meeting on schedule.

Record Keeping

Keeping track of group developments and decisions is vitally important for any group, whether local or spread out across an entire province. Why is it necessary to keep records? To make plans for your organization you need to know about the level of demand and how your support group is being used. What's actually happening in your group and are members feeling supported? Keeping track of group goings-on is also important for new members to see the evolution of the group. Also, if your support group decides to have a community event to raise money, you'll need to demonstrate that there's a need for what you are doing. Funders want to be assured before handing over money that they're supporting a great cause and enhancing community strength. That's why budgets are a critical component of your decision-making process. And to be useful they must be absolutely realistic. What can you realistically expect to bring in, in revenue over the next year, two, or three years? Not what you would wish for or even what you think you need or want, but what you can achieve.

Starting a support group can be lots of work. There's developing an interest among people, figuring out what your group's purpose is, planning meetings, and shaping an agenda to name a few. However, once it's up and running and others (including you) are around to delegate, it will certainly help with feeling less isolated, and eventually with accessing community resources.

DISCUSSION TOPICS

Here are some things that were identified by one grandparent support group as being important topics for discussion:

Economic difficulties related to affordable housing and childcare expenses

Lack of legal advice about guardianship, custody or adoption

Access to community support and information about how to enroll grandchildren in school; locate refresher courses in parenting, etc.

Emotional, psychological well-being of child and grandparent and parent

Dealing with physical health problems due to aging

Dealing with grandchild's parent(s) and other family members

Dealing with legal issues and government offices

Balancing work and child care

DISCUSSION TOPICS

Dealing with special needs grandchildren and the school system, and finding adequate services for grandchild's special needs such as Down syndrome, Attention Deficit Hyper-activity Disorder (ADHD), Fetal Alcohol Syndrome and attachment, etc.

Discipline, strategies and challenges

Lack of public awareness

Psychologists or therapists who can help them with childrearing issues and work directly with their grandchildren

Tutors who can help with a grandchild's educational needs

PLANNING FOR THE FUTURE

You can't stop the clock. It's just one of those things: children grow up, challenges or not. Transition periods[13] are typically hard, as both children and their parents adjust to growth, change and new developmental tasks. Further, some special needs conditions such as FASD make it particularly difficult for those affected to deal well with change.

You might remember, from the days when you were parenting the first time around, the passage from infancy to pre-school, pre-school to school years, or the pre-teens to adolescence. The transition from adolescence to adulthood has been noted as one of the most stressful times for many so-called typical families, and it is even harder for grandparents raising their grandchildren because of age, finances and the ever looming possibility of illness.

Look into Available Services
There are organizations that help families who are trying to plan ahead for their children or grandchildren who have special needs. For example, the Planned Lifetime Advocacy Network (PLAN) is a British Columbia-based organization that is committed to assisting Canadian families create a secure future for their children with disabilities. These organizations can help you with things like estate planning and building a personal support network for your grandchild. Talk to your social worker or local family centre for information on services in your area.

Examine Your Financial Resources
It's important that you organize your finances in the way that's most helpful to your grand-

---

[13]This section is taken, in part, from *Adoption Piece by Piece: Special Needs* (2003) published by Groundwork Press. Copies are available at www.groundworkpress.com.

child and to your estate. Trusts, RESPs and other types of savings can go a long way in preparing your grandchild for the future. See Part 2: Caregiver 101, Chapter 5: Systems for more detailed information on financial planning.

Create a Personal Support Network

It's important to plan for the care of your grandchild should you one day be unable to do so. Approach relatives and friends and find out how involved they are willing to be in your grandchild's life. Do this if she is still a minor, or if she is an adult with special needs that require attention. For example, if your grandchild is an adult with challenges and you become unable to care for her, your nephew may be willing to take care of legal and financial matters while a friend of the family might wish to help with groceries and meal preparation. You may also want to look into the possibility of setting money aside to hire a caregiver who will help your grandchild with day-to-day tasks. If your grandchild is still a minor, discuss as soon as possible with the trusted adults in her life who will be willing and able to take over parenting. It is these networks that will provide consistency and support in your absence.

Prepare Your Grandchild for Independent Living

As soon as it is appropriate, begin to teach your grandchild life skills that she will need when she is an adult. Start with the basics like cooking, grocery shopping and keeping track of money. Make sure you praise her progress in order to build self-esteem and give her a sense of ability. More complicated skills include how to act appropriately in different social situations, self-advocacy and managing her own health. The more you teach her now, the better prepared she will be when she is living independently.

Legal Decisions

If your grandchild has developmental disabilities or disabilities that affect cognitive functioning, you may wish to remove your child's rights and make all decisions for her. Be aware that this is complicated and strips your grandchild of all legal rights, which, when you are unable to care for her, may become a problem as she will not be able to make decisions regarding her own welfare. Look into other alternatives such as representation agreements, which allow your grandchild to choose one or more people to help make decisions about health and other matters.

Letting Go

Once you've confronted your fears and feelings around your grandchild's adulthood, and have done your best to put plans and early interventions in place, you ultimately have to let go. Let it be. After all, you can't stop the clock. Your grandchild will grow up. Letting go doesn't mean you can't revisit and revise your plans as needed. The trick is to adapt and adjust—something you're probably good at by now, having raised your grandchild in, sometimes, not the best of circumstances.

APPENDICES

GLOSSARY

Adoption
By adopting your grandchild, you become his or her parent and therefore have all the legal rights and obligations that a parent would have. Adoption only occurs after the parental rights of your grandchild's birth parents have been removed or voluntarily given up. The child may have been in foster care and legally in the custody of the child welfare authority after parental rights were removed because of a protection concern, or the birth parents may give up their parental rights specifically so you can adopt your grandchild.

Advocacy
Acting for yourself or on behalf of others to advance a cause or an idea, or to receive services you believe you are entitled to.

Burden of proof
In the case of a grandparent, this would come into play if the grandchild's parents refuse access to the child. Either party (the grandparent seeking access or the parent denying access) can initiate court proceedings. This would also come into play should the grandparent decide to sue the parent for custody. In family court, the main test is what is in the best interests of the child. This is completely separate from the wishes of the parent or grandparent.

Canada child tax benefit
This is a monthly, tax-free payment made to some families to help them with the cost of raising children under age 18. The benefit may also include the National Child Benefit Supplement or the child Disability Benefit.

Child in care

This means that the child is in the care of the government and that the province or state has the legal authority to make decisions on the child's behalf as well as the legal responsibility to take care of the child. This may mean that the child is in foster care with a non-relative, or is living with a grandparent in kinship care or a restricted foster home that is monitored by child welfare social workers.

Custody of a child

This term comes up most often when parents divorce (or separate in a common law situation) and there is a question as to who will care for the child. If a grandparent becomes the child's legal guardian or adopts the child, then he or she would have custody.

Foster care

This is care provided to children who are unable to live with their parents, usually because of a child protection concern. Grandparents, other relatives or friends of the family may become foster parents for a particular child (their arrangement with the child welfare authorities is sometimes called a restricted foster home) and receive benefits and funding close or equal to that of other foster care providers. Foster parents are paid by childcare services to parent temporarily. However, if the biological parents' rights are terminated by a court or are given up voluntarily, foster parents may sometimes adopt the child if the adoption authorities decide it's in the best interest of the child. The child may also be adopted by a family not associated with foster care.

Developmental disabilities

This term refers to a chronic disability that is linked to a mental or physical impairment or a combination of both. Developmental disabilities include conditions such as Down's syndrome and autism.

Grief and loss

This combination of feelings—sadness, emptiness, anger, loneliness and despair—comes into play for many life events that are connected to loss (i.e. death of loved one, loss of a job, divorce). Experiencing these emotions, which are referred to, in combination, as grieving, is a necessary stage toward coming to terms with loss.

Guardian

This refers to the person who is responsible for the care and control of a child. You may eventually obtain custody or arrange for custody of the child with someone else if, for example, both parents pass away and a friend may be the immediate guardian as per the will, even though the child will eventually be placed in the custody of a relative such as a grandparent.

Home study
In the case of an adoption, the home study is a written assessment of the adoptive family by a licensed social worker who specializes in adoption. This worker can sometimes be chosen by the potential adoptive family. The purpose of the home study is to make sure that a child is placed in a stable, loving home. It also gives the family an opportunity to talk about and explore adoption issues before the process is finalized.

In-care placement
The government has custody or guardianship of the child and places the child either with relatives or a foster family.

Individual education plan (IEP)
This plan is used to help a child who may be having difficulty in school. The IEP outlines the goals the team of educators and caregivers have set for the child, along with any special supports required to help achieve these goals.

Informal kinship care
This occurs when the child is being cared for by next of kin but does not have *in-care status* with childcare services. Often, these arrangements are private and organized between relatives or family friends without the involvement of child welfare authorities. Sometimes, these arrangements are also organized by social workers as an alternative to paid foster care and continued government involvement.

Interests of the child test
Courts use this to decide who will care for a child according to his or her best interests. Factors considered by the court to decide the best interests of a child include: age and sex of the child, child's mental and physical health, parent's mental and physical health, lifestyle of the parents, relationship between the parents and the child, ability of the parents to provide the child with food, shelter, and clothing, established living pattern for the child concerning school, home, and community, and the child's preference.

In loco parentis
Translated literally, *in loco parentis* means "in place of a parent." This term is used to describe a custody arrangement, like when grandparents have served as a custodial parent for the child for a significant period of time and have cared for the child in the place of a birth parent.

Kinship care

This type of care includes caregivers who are parents, siblings or other relatives, and those who aren't necessarily related by blood, but are important to the child. If the child is in government care, or needs protection, a kinship care arrangement might occur through the foster care system. If the government has never been involved, then this could also take the form of an informal kinship care arrangement.

Kith and Kin agreement

This written agreement based in British Columbia is between the child welfare authority and a child's extended family member such as a grandparent, or other person known to the child. The agreement enables the person to care for the child and usually, but not always, outlines the financial support the government will provide to the proposed caregiver. The child is not under government care and the birth parent remains the legal guardian. The parent agrees to this arrangement and is involved in the child's care plan. A social worker may check up on the child, but since a Kith and Kin agreement is not monitored by foster care, government involvement is minimal.

Legal custody

A legal status created by court order which gives the grandparent various, parent-like rights and duties such as providing food, shelter, clothing, medical care and education. It also includes keeping the child safe, disciplining the child, as well as living with the child in the same household. Custody does not mean that the grandparent has adopted the child.

Multigenerational household

This refers to a household in which at least three generations live, usually grandparents, parents and grandchildren.

Open adoption

An adoption where there is still some contact between the birth family, adoptive family, and the child. Sometimes foster families are also involved. Open adoptions are often regulated by openness agreements, which is an agreement between the birth family and adoptive family that outlines the kind of relationship they will have.

Out-of-care

This refers to a situation where the child is never officially in care, but is instead being cared for by grandparents or other caregivers through a private arrangement.

Parental rights

Along with those rights and duties included in legal custody, parental rights and duties include the duty to support and provide necessities of life. The parents of children in foster care or kinship care generally will not have had their parental rights removed. Once parental rights have been terminated, the child is often adopted, sometimes by grandparents or other relatives, or by a different family altogether.

Peace bond
In Canadian law this refers to an order from criminal court that limits one person from bothering or threatening another. A peace bond is only issued when there has been some involvement with the criminal justice system. Typically, peace bonds are issued when someone fears for his or her safety or the safety of a dependent, usually a child, based on a single incident of a history of incidents. The bond can last for up to twelve months.

Respite care
This term refers to the temporary or short-term care of a child by adults other than the primary caregivers. This form of care exists so that the caregivers can have some time away from the child in order to allow them to "regroup" and prepare once again for the daily challenges of parenting.

Restraining order
An order from a family (civil) court directing one person not to do something, such as contact another person, enter the family home or remove a child from the geographical area. Restraining orders can be issued in family court and are not necessarily limited to preventing criminal activity.

Skipped generation families
A family where the parents are absent from the home and grandparents step in to care for the child.

Visitation rights
The right granted by a court to a parent or other relative who doesn't have custody of a child to visit the child on a regular basis.

Talking circle
A talking circle, traditionally used in Aboriginal cultures, is a gathering of people who come together to talk about a certain issue or to express feelings or thoughts that are normally kept private. A sacred object, commonly an eagle feather or a stick, is passed around the circle to everyone who wishes to speak. While the speaker is holding the sacred object, he or she can speak for as long as he or she needs to and on any subject, and cannot be interrupted by other participants. The purpose of the talking circle is so that participants

can unclutter their feelings and thoughts and express themselves freely and without fear. Talking circles are often used as forms of support groups by tribal councils, Aboriginal friendship centres and other First Nations organizations.

Permanency
Permanency is the approach that looks at the most suitable, permanent home for a child, including, but not limited to, relatives, adoption, guardianship, or independent living. This term is used most often by social workers who are planning a child's future.

Registered education savings plan (RESP)
This is a financial planning tool that grandparents or other adults can contribute to over several years in order to save for a child's post-secondary education. Like a RRSP, tax is not paid on the earned interest until the RESP is cashed in. Contributions are tax deductible at the time of deposit. The Canadian government provides top-ups to RESP contributions, up to $400 per year per child.

Registered retirement savings plan (RRSP)
This is a plan that allows individuals to contribute to retirement funds over several years. Earned interest cannot be taxed until the RRSP is cashed in. The limits one can contribute to a RRSP are based on annual income. Contributions are tax deductible at the time of deposit.

Special needs
This is an umbrella term for an array of physical, mental, emotional, or developmental challenges that often call for extra supports and services such as special education or medical equipment. The individual with special needs may need assistance with the tasks of daily living.

Subsidized housing
This refers to housing in which the government provides some type of subsidy or rent assistance to the family living. Subsidized housing includes public, not-for-profit and co-operative housing.

Temporary care assistance program
Temporary care assistance (available only in Ontario) is financial support offered to an adult who is looking after a child in financial need in the absence of a parent. This program is administered by Ontario Works and can pay up to $270 per month per child.

Therapist

A therapist is a professional (i.e. psychologist, psychiatrist or counsellor) who is trained to help individuals work out difficulties in their lives that cause emotional and psychological distress.

Time-out

This is a discipline technique where the caregiver directs the child to a quiet place to calm down after an outburst or inappropriate behaviour. The duration of time-outs depends on the developmental age of the child (some parenting guides suggest one minute for every year of the child's life). Afterward, the caregiver discusses with the child the reasons behind his behaviour and alternative ways of expressing anger or other emotions.

Trust fund

This is an amount of money that a person places in the custody of a trustee to be used for the benefit of the child, who is called the beneficiary. The money in a trust fund is usually given to the child in adulthood, often at a significant birthday or when the child graduates from school.

Will

A document in which a person specifies what is to be done with his or her property after death. You can also use your will to name a guardian for the grandchildren whom you live with so that they will be cared for after you die.

RESOURCES

Books and Articles

Callahan, Marilyn, Leslie Brown, Patricia McKenzie and Barbara Whittington. "Knitting up the ravelled sleeve of care: Grandmothers making families with their grandchildren" *Family Making: Towards Inclusive and Anti-oppressive Research and Practice with Families.* Family Making Collective, 2006. Available at http://www.ucs.mun.ca/%7Elbella2/family_making.html.

> This study of nine Canadian grandmothers explores the challenges and joys of parenting a second time.

Cowan, Lissa and Jennifer Lee. *Living with Prenatal Drug Exposure: A Guide for Parents.* Vancouver, British Columbia: Groundwork Press, 2003.

> This comprehensive book for parents and professionals introduces caregivers to the challenges of caring for a child prenatally exposed to drugs. The guide offers practical techniques and strategies, debunks well-known myths, explores social issues and includes a workbook section for parents and other caregivers.

DeToledo, Sylvie and Deborah Edler Brown. *Grandparents as Parents: A Survival Guide for Raising a Second Family.* New York: Guilford Press, 1995.

> This is a practical guide for caregiver grandparents. It includes tips on parenting, exploring issues such as grief and loss, and further topics for discussion.

Falk, Ursula Adler and Gerhard Falk. *Grandparents: A New Look at the Supporting Generation.* Amherst, NY: Prometheus Books, 2002.

> This book looks at who grandparents have become in the 21st century.

Fuller-Thomson, Esme. "Grandparents Raising Grandchildren in Canada: A Profile of Skipped Generation Families." *SEDAP—a Program for Research on Social and Economic Dimensions of an Aging Population.* Hamilton, Ontario: McMaster University, October 2005.

> Using data from the 1996 Canadian Census, this paper presents a profile of grandparents raising grandchildren in skipped generation households.

Graefe, Sara. *Living with FASD: A Guide for Parents.* Vancouver, British Columbia: Groundwork Press, 2003.

> Bringing up-to-date and comprehensive information about FASD, this book includes the latest Institute of Medicine diagnostic criteria and terms, special considerations for infants and adolescents, parent needs, and an expanded resource list.

Graefe, Sara. Ed. *Adoption Piece by Piece: Lifelong Issues, Special Needs, A Toolkit for Parents* (3 vols). Vancouver: Groundwork Press. 2003.

> This three-volume set covers everything from adopting a child who has Fetal Alcohol Spectrum Disorder (FASD) to receiving the help your child needs from his or her family doctor or teacher. This series represents a comprehensive collection of articles from experienced parents and professionals on a variety of topics related to adoption.

Jarratt, Claudia Jewett. *Helping Children Cope with Separation and Loss.* Boston: Harvard Common Press, 1994.

> A sensitive and practical guide to helping children with grief and loss issues related to separation, divorce, death, adoption and other concerns.

Kruk, E. (1995). "Grandparent-Grandchild Contact Loss: Findings from a Study of 'Grandparent Rights' Members," *Canadian Journal on Aging* 14 (3), 737-754 (Canadian Association on Gerontology).

> Kruk, E. and Hall, B. (1995). "The Disengagement of Paternal Grandparents Subsequent to Divorce," *Journal of Divorce and Remarriage* 23 (1/2), 131-147 (Haworth Press).

> Kruk, E. (1994). "Grandparent Visitation Disputes: Multigenerational Approaches to Family Mediation," *Mediation Quarterly* 12 (1), 37-53 (Academy of Family Mediators/ Jossey-Bass Publishers).

> These three studies provide useful insight into the social trends and challenges that affect grandparents who are dealing with visitation and custody.

Neufeld, Gordon and Gabor Maté. *Hold on to Your Kids: Why Parents Need to Matter.* Toronto: Knopf Canada, 2004.

A practical book for parents and grandparents who are struggling to maintain strong relationships with their children in the face of social and peer influences.

Reid, Gayla. *The Child's Right to Love.* People's Law School in partnership with the Canadian Grandparents Rights Association, BC branch. May 2001. Vancouver, BC. www. publiclegaled.bc.ca.

Information for grandparents, relatives, and others close to the child. This publication explains the rights of those who want to maintain a relationship with a child after there has been a separation of the parents or other event.

Watkins, Kathleen Pullan and Lucius Durant Jr. *Working with Children and Families Affected by Substance Abuse.* West Nyack, NY: Center for Applied Research in Education.

This resource outlines the effects of drugs and alcohol on children, and resulting issues for families.

Wright, Pam and Pete Wright. *From Emotions to Advocacy: The Special Education Survival Guide.* Hartfield, VA: Harbor House Law Press, 2001.

This practical, step-by-step guide teaches caregivers effective advocacy tools and strategies to be used in securing special education programs and services.

Organizations and Agencies

Aboriginal Canada Portal
www.aboriginalcanada.gc.ca
1-800-399-0111
ACP@inac.gc.ca

This online portal provides visitors with Canadian Aboriginal online resources, contacts, information, and federal and provincial government programs and services. It connects people to Aboriginal associations, businesses, organizations, bands, communities, groups, news and peoples.

Aboriginal Infant Development Programs of BC
Suite 200-506 Fort Street
Victoria, BC V8W 1E6
250-388-5593
www.aido.bc.ca

> Aboriginal Infant Development Programs in British Columbia offer support to families of infants who are at risk for or have been diagnosed with developmental delays. Programs are voluntary, family centered, and primarily focused on children ages 0-3 (in some communities 0 - 6).

BC Aboriginal Child Care Society
708-100 Park Royal South
West Vancouver, BC V7T 1A2
604-913-9128
www.acc-society.bc.ca
reception@acc-society.bc.ca

> The BC Aboriginal Child Care Society is a non-profit charitable society serving Aboriginal early childhood programs throughout British Columbia.

Canadian Association for Community Living
Kinsmen Building, York University
4700 Keele Street
Toronto, ON M3J 1P3
416-661-9611
www.cacl.ca
inform@cacl.ca

> The Canadian Association for Community Living is a Canada-wide association of family members and others working for the benefit of persons of all ages who have an intellectual disability.

Canadian Centre on Substance Abuse
75 Albert Street, Suite 300
Ottawa, ON K1P 5E7
613-235-4048
www.ccsa.ca

> The CCSA promotes informed debate on substance abuse issues and encourages public participation in reducing the harm associated with drug abuse; disseminates information on the nature, extent and consequences of substance abuse; and sup-

ports and assists organizations involved in substance abuse treatment, prevention and educational programming.

Canadian Grandparents' Rights Association
207-14980 104th Avenue
Surrey, BC V3R 1M9
604-585-8242
cgra222@vcn.bc.ca

Promotes, supports, and assists grandparents and their families in maintaining or re-establishing family ties and stability when the family has been disrupted. Focuses on the ties between grandparents and grandchildren. Offers information, peer counselling, and support groups across BC.

Canadian Mental Health Association
www.cmha.ca

The CMHA exists to promote mental health and to serve mental health consumers, their families and friends. Visit the website for a list of regional locations.

Canada Revenue Agency
www.cra-arc.gc.ca

The Canada Revenue Agency (CRA) administers tax laws for the Government of Canada and for most provinces and territories along with various social and economic benefit and incentive programs delivered through the tax system. For a list of local tax service offices go to www.cra-arc.gc.ca/contact/tso-e.html. To find out what tax benefits and requirements apply to Aboriginal peoples you can visit www.cra-arc.gc.ca/aboriginals.

CANGRANDS National Kinship Support
R.R. 1
McArthurs Mills, ON K0L 2M0
613-474-0035
www.cangrands.com
gradma@cangrands.com

CANGRANDS assists the special needs of kin-headed households by advocating for the best interests of all children in our care. Manages support groups across Canada.

CH.A.D.D. Canada
Children and Adults with Attention Deficit Disorders
1376 Bank Street
Ottawa, ON K1H 7Y3
613-731-1209
www.chaddcanada.org
info@chaddcanada.org

> CH.A.D.D. Canada is a not-for-profit parent-run organization that aims to help support, educate and better the lives of individuals with ADD and those who care for them. They have chapters in communities across Canada where meetings are held.

Department of Indian and Northern Affairs
www.ainc-inac.gc.ca

> INAC is responsible for Indian and Inuit Affairs and Northern Affairs. INAC's responsibilities encompass a broad range of services related to employment education, treaties and status. A list of regional offices can be found online at www.ainc-inac.gc.ca/ro/index_e.html.

Assistant Deputy Minister's Office
First Nations and Inuit Health Branch
Health Canada
Jeanne Mance Building, Tunney's Pasture
Postal Locator 1921A
Ottawa, Ontario K1A 0K9
613 957-7700
www.hc-sc.gc.ca/fnih-spni/index_e.html
fnihb-dgspni@hc-sc.gc.ca

> The First Nations and Inuit Health Branch of Health Canada works with First Nations people and Inuit on issues related to health. A list of branches in your area can be found online at www.hc-sc.gc.ca/home-accueil/contact/fnih-spni/rd-dr_e.html. This branch also offers a list of drug treatment locations throughout Canada.

Griefworks BC
4500 Oak St. Rm. E405
Vancouver, BC V6H 3N1
604-875-2741
person@griefworksbc.com
www.griefworksbc.com

> Griefworks BC's main objective is to provide grief support to children, teens and

adults in need of information and resources. Website includes links and grief support chat room.

Helping Spirit Lodge Society
3965 Dumfries Street
Vancouver, BC V5N 5R3
604 872-6649
helping_spirit@telus.net
> This Society addresses the issues of Aboriginal family violence from a holistic perspective.

Indian Residential School Survivors Society
911-100 Park Royal South
West Vancouver, BC V7T 1A2
604-925-4464
1-866-925-4419 (24 hour crisis line)
www.irsss.ca
> Assists First Peoples in British Columbia to recognize and be holistically empowered from the primary and generational effects of residential schools by supporting research, promoting awareness, establishing partnerships and advocating for justice and healing and by supporting survivors through crisis counselling, court support, information, referrals, training and education workshops.

Kla-how-eya Aboriginal Centre of SACS
13629-108th Avenue
Surrey, BC V3T 2K4
www.sacsbc.org
pmason@sacs.bc.org
> The society supports activities that promote the health and economic well being of Aboriginal peoples, and promotes the resurgence of resident Aboriginal culture, language and teachings, particularly those of local nations residing within the traditional territories.

Learning Disabilities Association of Canada
323 Chapel Street
Ottawa, ON K1N 7Z2
613-238-5721
www.ldac.taac.ca
information@ldac-taac.ca

> This is the national association for people with learning disabilities and those who support them. LDAC has provincial chapters and groups in local communities as well.

The People's Law School
150-900 Howe Street
Vancouver BC V6Z 2M4
604-331-5400
www.publiclegaled.bc.ca

> A non-profit, non-partisan public legal education organization that reaches British Columbians who would not otherwise have access to the legal education and information they need.

PLAN—The Planned Lifetime Advocacy Network
260-3665 Kingsway
Vancouver, BC V5R 5W2
604-439-9566
www.plan.ca
inquiries@plan.ca

> PLAN helps families secure the future for their relative with a disability through support, financial planning and community.

BIBLIOGRAPHY

"Age-standardized mortality rates by selected causes." *Vital Statistics.* 2004. Statistics Canada. September 14, 2006 http://www40.statcan.ca/l01/cst01/health30a.htm.

Benton, Mark. "Letter to Ted Hughes." *LSS News Releases.* 2006. Legal Services Society of British Columbia. 14 August 2006 <http://www.lss.bc.ca/assets/about_lss/Hughes_submission.pdf>.

Bowlby, John. *Attachment.* New York: Basic Books, 1971.

---. *Separation: Anxiety & Anger.* New York: Basic Books, 1973.

---. *Loss: Sadness & Depression.* New York: Basic Books, 1980.

Callahan, Marilyn, Leslie Brown, Patricia McKenzie and Barbara Whittington. "Knitting up the ravelled sleeve of care: Grandmothers making families with their grandchildren" *Family Making: Towards Inclusive and Anti-oppressive Research and Practice with Families.* 2006. Family Making Collective. 14 August 2006 <http://www.ucs.mun.ca/~lbella2/chapter15.htm>.

---. "The Underground Child Welfare System: Grandmothers Raising Grandchildren." *Perspectives* 27.5 (2005): 12-13.

Canada. Department of Justice. Family and Youth Section. *Grandparent-Grandchild Access, a Legal Analysis.* Ottawa: Queens's Printer, 2003.

"Checkups and Prevention." *AARP.* 2006. AARP. 14 August 2006 <http://www.aarp.org/health/staying_healthy/prevention>.

"Child and Family Development Service Standards." *Ministry of Children and Family Development.* 2004. Province of British Columbia. 14 August 2006 <http://www.mcf.gov.bc.ca/child_protection/pdf/cfd_ss_july04.pdf>.

"Child in home of a Relative (CIHR)." *Ministry of Employment and Income Assistance.* 2003. Province of British Columbia. 3 August 2006 <http://www.gov.bc.ca/bvprd/bc/or/programView.do?programPage=/or/programBody.jsp&progView=items&navId=NAV_ID_mhr

&programId=536882875&channelId=-536893799&expandChannelId=-536893786&brwId=%402Id1US%7C0YQtuW&crumb=B.C.+Home&crumburl=%2Fhome.do#>.

Climo, J.J., Terry Patterson and Kim Lay. "Using the double bind to interpret the experience of custodial grandparents." *Journal of Aging Studies* 16 (2002): 19-35.

Cowan, Lissa. "Take Care or Else: Relearning How to Breathe." *Family Groundwork* 20.3 (2004): 13.

Cowan, Lissa and Jennifer Lee. *Living with Prenatal Drug Exposure: A Guide for Parents.* Vancouver: Groundwork Press, 2003.

Dannison, Linda L. and Andrea B. Smith. "Custodial Grandparents Community Support Program: Lessons Learned." *Children and Schools* 25.2 (2003): 87-95.

---. "Grandparent-headed families in the United States." *Journal of Intergenerational Relationships* 1.3 (2003): 35-47.

Davies, Curt. "The Grandparent Study 2002 Report." *AARP Policy and Research.* 2002. AARP. 31 August 2006 <http://www.aarp.org/research/family/grandparenting/aresearch-import-481.html>.

---. "Lean on Me, Support and Minority Outreach for Grandparents Raising Grandchildren." *AARP Policy and Research.* September 2003. AARP. 5 September 2006 <http://www.aarp.org/research/family/grandparenting/aresearch-import-483.html>.

DeToledo, Sylvie and Deborah Edler Brown. *Grandparents as Parents: A Survival Guide for Raising a Second Family.* New York: Guilford Press, 1995.

Doucette-Dudman, Deborah and Jeffrey R. LaCure. *Raising our Children's Children.* Minneapolis: Fairview Press, 1996.

Falk, Ursula Adler and Gerhard Falk. *Grandparents: A New Look at the Supporting Generation.* Amherst, NY: Prometheus Books, 2002.

Fuller-Thomson, Esme and Meredith Minkler. "American Grandparents Providing Extensive Child Care to Their Grandchildren: Prevalence and Profile." *The Gerontologist* 41.2 (2001): 201-209

---. "Notes from Focus Group held at the Salvation Army Camp." E-mail to Jennifer Lee from Betty Cornelius. 26 September 2006.

---. "Grandparents Raising Grandchildren in Canada: A Profile of Skipped Generation Families." *SEDAP—a Program for Research on Social and Economic Dimensions of an Aging Population.* Hamilton, Ontario: McMaster University, October 2005.

"Financial Support." *Cangrands.* 2006. Cangrands. 2 August 2006 <http://www.cangrands.com/grgsupport.htm>.

Glass, J. Conrad and Terry L. Huneycutt. "Grandparents Parenting Grandchildren: Extent of Situation, Issues Involved, and Educational Implications." *Educational Gerontology* 28 (2002): 139-161.

Goodman, Catherine Chase and Merril Silverstein. "Grandmothers who Parent their Grandchildren: An Exploratory Study of Close Relations across Three Generations." *Journal of Family Issues* 22.5 (2001): 557-558.

Gilmore, Ruby, Sherryl Bohna, Da Wen and Joanne Boley. "Diversity Group Project:

Grandparents Raising Grandchildren." *Cangrands*. 2005. Cangrands. 11 August 2006 <www.cangrands.com/download. htm>.

Graefe, Sara. Ed. *Adoption Piece by Piece: Lifelong Issues, Special Needs, A Toolkit for Parents* (3 vols). Vancouver: Groundwork Press, 2003.

---. *Living with FASD: A Guide for Parents.* Vancouver: Groundwork Press, 2003.

---. "You're Never Too Old: the Joys and Challenges of Adoption for Older Parents." *Adoption Piece by Piece: Lifelong Issues.* Vancouver: Groundwork Press, 2003. 199.

Grandparenting Again in Canada. July 2005. Ontario Association of Children's Aid Societies. 3 October 2006 <http://www. grandparentingagaincanada.com/kinship-care.htm>.

"Grandparent-Grandchild Access, a Legal Analysis." 2003. Prepared by Dan L. Goldberg for Family Child and Youth Section, Department of Justice, Canada. 14 August 2006 <http://www.canada. justice.gc.ca/en/ps/pad/reports/2003-FCY-15E.pdf>.

Grant, Roy. "The Special Needs of Children in Kinship Care." *Grandparents as Carers of Children with Disabilities, Facing the Challenges.* Eds. Philip McCallion and Mathew Janicki. New York: The Haworth Press, 2000. 17-34.

Grinstead, Leder and Bond Jensen. "Review of Research on the Health of Caregiving Grandparents." *Journal of Advanced Nursing* 44.3 (2000): 318-326.

Guzell-Roe, Jacqueline R., Jean M. Gerard and Laura Landry-Meyer. "Custodial Grandparents' Perceived Control over Caregiving Outcomes: Raising Children the Second time Around." *Journal of Intergenerational Relationships* 3.2 (2005): 43-61.

Hagen, Stanley B. "Safety, Well-Being Focus of Child Protection System." *Ministry of Children and Family Development.* 2005. Province of British Columbia. 14 August 2006 <http://www.bcchildprotection. ca/05nov22_hagen_statement.htm>.

Harrison, Kelley A., Gina S. Richman and Glenda L. Vittimberga. "Parental Stress in Grandparents Versus Parents Raising Children With Behaviour Problems." *Journal of Family Issues* 21.2 (2000): 262-270.

Hayslip, Bert and Patricia L. Kaminski. "Grandparents Raising Their Grandchildren: A Review of the Literature and Suggestions for Practice." *The Gerontologist* 45.2 (2005): 262-269.

"Help for Grandparents Raising Grandchildren." *AARP.* 2006. AARP. 28 September 2006. http://www.aarp.org/families/grandparents/raising_grandchild/a2004-01-16-findinghelp.html.

"Housing Issues When Grandchildren Move In." *AARP.* 2006. AARP. 28 July 2006 <http://www.aarp.org/families/grandparents/raising_grandchild/a2004-09-01-grandparents-housingissues.html>.

"Issue: Kinship Care." *Grandparenting Again Canada.* 2006. Grandparenting Again Canada. 2 August 2006 <http://www. grandparentingagaincanada.com/kinship-care.htm>.

Jarratt, Claudia Jewett. *Helping Children Cope with Separation and Loss*. Boston: Harvard Common Press, 1994.

Kerr, Ann. "Grandparents Shouldn't Forget Selves." *The Globe and Mail* 18 February 2004: F4.

---. "Raising a Family—Again." *The Globe and Mail* 18 February 2004: F1.

Kolomer, Stacey. "Kinship Foster Care and its Impact on Grandmother Caregivers." *Grandparents as Carers of Children with Disabilities, Facing the Challenges*. Eds. Philip McCallion and Mathew Janicki. New York: The Haworth Press, 2000. 57-84.

Kropf, P. Nancy and Margaret M. Robinson."Pathways into Caregiving for Rural Custodial Grandparents." *Journal of Intergenerational Relationships* 2.1 (2004): 63-77.

Lee, Jennifer. "It's Your Health Too: Preventing Caregiver Burnout." *Family Groundwork* 20.3 (2004): 12.

---. "Parenting the Second Time Around: How to Deal with Grandparent Adoption." *Adoption Piece by Piece, Lifelong Issues*. Vancouver, Groundwork press, 2003. 197.

Levine, Melvin D., William B. Carey and Allen C. Crocker, eds. *Developmental-Behavioural Pediatrics*. 2nd ed. Philadelphia: WB Saunders, 1992.

Milan, Anne and Brian Hamm. "Across the Generations: Grandparents and Grandchildren." *Canadian Social Trends* 11-008. Ottawa: Statistics Canada, 2003.

Minkler, Meredith. "Survey of Grandparents Reveals Stress of Caring for Grandchildren." *Vulnerable Populations*. 2002. Robert Wood Johnson Foundation. 1 October 2006 <http://www.rwjf.org/portfolios/resources/grantsreport.jsp?filename=035181.htm&iaid=144>.

Morley, Jane. "Heshook-ish Tsawalk: Towards a State of Healthy Interdependence in the Child Welfare System." *Ministry of Children and Family Development*. 2006. Province of British Columbia. 28 July 2006 <http://www.gov.bc.ca/cyo/down/heshook_ish_tsawalk_special_report.pdf>.

Muggeridge, Peter. "Beyond Loving." *CARP Magazine*. 2006. 50Plus. 1 October 2006 <http://en.50plus.com/display.cfm?documentID=9394&CabinetID=369&LibraryID=112>.

Muldoon, Paul. "Grandparents Raising Grandchildren in Simcoe County. Barrie and District Association for People with Special Needs and Grands Parenting Again support group." *Cangrands*. 2003. Cangrands. 28 July 2006 <www.cangrands.com/printpages/grgrfinalreport2003.pdf>.

Nolo, your legal companion. 2006. Nolo. 5 October 2006 <http://www.nolo.com>.

Rosenthal, Carolyn J. and James Gladstone. "Grandparenthood in Canada." *Contemporary Family Trends*. 2001. Vanier Institute of the Family. 28 July 2006 <http://www.vifamily.ca/library/cft/grandparenthood.html>.

Schmid, Jeannette, Ruth Tansony, Sandra Goranson and Darlene Sykes. "Family Group Conferencing: Doorway to Kinship Care."*OACAS Journal* 48.4 (2004): 2-7.

Shimshon M. Neikrug. "A New Grandparenting: Dialogue and Covenant Through Grandparenting." *Grandparents as Carers of Children with Disabilities, Facing the Challenges.* Eds. McCallion, Philip and Mathew Janicki. New York: The Haworth Press, 2000. 17-34.

Staudacher, Carol. *Beyond Grief: a Guide for Recovering from the Death of a Loved One.* Oakland, CA: New Harbinger Publications, 1987.

"Temporary Care Assistance." *Ontario Works.* 2001. Ontario Ministry of Community and Social Services. 9 August 2006. <http://www.mcss.gov.on.ca/mcss/english/pillars/social/ow-directives/ow_policy_directives.htm>.

Truly, Traci. *Grandparents Rights with Forms.* Clearwater, Florida: Sphinx Publishing, 1995.

Watkins, Kathleen Pullan and Lucius Durant Jr. *Working with Children and Families Affected by Substance Abuse.* West Nyack, NY: Center for Applied Research in Education, 1996.

Whitley, Deborah M., Susan J. Kelley and Theresa Ann Sipe. "Grandmothers Raising Grandchildren: Are They at Increased Risk of Health Problems?" *Health and Social Work* 26.2 (2001): 105-114.

Wright, Pam and Pete Wright. *From Emotions to Advocacy: The Special Education Survival Guide.* Hartfield, VA: Harbor House Law Press, 2001.

Watson, Brad. "Setting Up Your Support Group: A Guide for Parents." *Adoption Piece by Piece, a Toolkit for Parents.* Vancouver: Groundwork Press, 2003.123.

ACKNOWLEDGEMENTS

As always, any book project involves many people and *Living with Your Grandchildren* is no exception.

Special thanks are in order for our generous and thoughtful review panel: Betty Cornelius, founder and president of CANGRANDS National Kinship Support and a caregiver grandparent herself; Barbara Whittington, Associate Professor in the School of Social Work at the University of Victoria; Kathryn Basran of the family law firm Schuman Daltrop Basran and Robin, Edward Kruk, Associate Professor in the School of Social Work and Family Studies at the University of British Columbia; and Carol Kersbergen, a caregiver grandparent who helped us understand the lives and feelings of grandparents just like her. We'd also like to thank Ginger Jones of the Kla-how-eya Aboriginal Centre for giving us valuable insight into First Nations' philosophies of grandparenthood and the challenges facing Aboriginal grandparents today.

And, of course, we can't forget Brad Watson and Verna Booth who guided us through the development, research and writing of *Living with Your Grandchildren* and were always available to hear and comment on our ideas. Thanks also to Myron Wealr for his practical turn of mind, which was sorely needed more than once!

And last, but not least, we'd like to thank the grandparents across Canada who patiently submitted to our interviews and provided honest answers to difficult and intimate questions. So, Ina, Ralph, Barbara, Karen and Val—thank you very, very much.

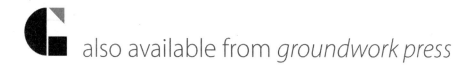
also available from *groundwork press*

Adoption Piece by Piece (3 volumes):
> **Lifelong Issues**
> **Special Needs**
> **A Toolkit for Parents**

Edited by Sara Graefe

This series represents a comprehensive collection of articles from experienced parents and professionals on a variety of topics related to adoption.

Living with Prenatal Drug Exposure: A Guide for Parents
By Lissa Cowan and Jennifer Lee

This comprehensive book for parents and professionals introduces caregivers to the challenges of caring for a child prenatally exposed to drugs.

Living with FASD: A Guide for Parents, 3rd Edition
By Sara Graefe

This updated 3rd edition includes diagnostic criteria, special considerations for infants and adolescents, and an expanded resource list.

Adoptive Families are Families for Keeps
Text by Lissa Cowan, illustrations by Stephanie Hill

This colouring book will provide social workers, foster parents, caregivers and educators with dynamic and instructive ways to introduce and discuss a wide range of adoption issues with young children.

Tara's Guide to Adoptive Families are Families for Keeps (CD-rom)
Text by Lissa Cowan and Jennifer Lee, animation by Dia Media

This companion CD-rom to *Adoptive Families are Families for Keeps* guides professionals and caregivers through over 50 relevant exercises and discussion topics to use together with the activity book.

Also available: *Fetal Alcohol Syndrome Support Group: A Six Module Curriculum, Professional Resource Kit: A Special Needs and Adoption Guide for Professionals, Family Groundwork* magazine and a selection of **FASD awareness brochures** for your next outreach project.

To order any of these titles, please visit our website at **www.groundworkpress.com**.